AUTISM

Medical and Educational Aspects

Second Edition

Autism

Medical and Educational Aspects

SECOND EDITION

T. PEETERS
Opleidingscentrum Autisme
Antwerp

C. GILLBERG, MD
University of Göteborg

W

WHURR PUBLISHERS

LONDON

First edition published by Janssen 1995
Second edition first published 1999 by
Whurr Publishers Ltd
19b Compton Terrace
London N1 2UN
England

Reprinted 1999, 2000, 2003 and 2004

British Library Cataloguing in Publication Data
A catalogue record for this book is available from the British Library.

ISBN 1 86156 093 1

Printed and bound in the UK by Athenaeum Press Ltd, Gateshead, Tyne & Wear.

Contents

Introduction   vii

Chapter 1   1

AUTISM AS A SYNDROME OF HYPERREALISM
Steven, Sven and the others–An apple and an orange–
Mistähänpitääeniten–The hyperrealists

Chapter 2   9

AUTISM AS A DEVELOPMENTAL DISORDER
The significant developmental scales–The even more significant
stories–The special story of people with Asperger syndrome–Outcome

Chapter 3   27

THE MEDICAL DIAGNOSIS OF AUTISM AND
DISORDERS OF THE AUTISM SPECTRUM
Classic autism, or Kanner syndrome–Disorders of the autism
spectrum–Differential diagnosis–A constantly recurring difficulty:
IQ–Neuropsychological testing–The incidence of autism in the population

Chapter 4   41

THE BIOLOGICAL BASIS OF AUTISM
Autism seldom occurs alone–Possible causal factors–Morphological and
biochemical signs of brain dysfunction–Putting one's finger on the
problem–A provisional synthesis–Conclusions

Chapter 5   49

EDUCATION AND GUIDANCE OF PEOPLE WITH AUTISM:
THE MEDICAL VIEWPOINT
The need for a structure–Frequent medical problems–Problems associated
with specific syndromes of the autism spectrum–Medication

Chapter 6   59

EDUCATION AND GUIDANCE OF PEOPLE WITH AUTISM:
THE MAJOR EDUCATIONAL STARTING POINTS
Herman, behavioural problems and the myth of Procrustes–Jan and the
limited power of abstraction–More on the level of abstraction–Maria and
the language trap

Chapter 7   71

TRAINING PROFESSIONALS AND PARENTS IN AUTISM
Autism is special in a special way–The triad–A pervasive developmental
disorder–The content of training–Types of training–Training
parents–Extraordinary youngsters require extraordinary professionals

Chapter 8   85

EDUCATION AND GUIDANCE OF PEOPLE WITH AUTISM:
PRACTICAL EXAMPLES
Where?–When? – How long?–Communication–Self-help and domestic
skills–Work skills and work behaviour–Leisure skills–Social skills –
Conclusions

Epilogue   115

References   117

Index   120

Introduction

Why does he never look me in the eyes with love and affection? Why does he laugh when I cry, instead of crying with me or asking why I am so sad? Why is he so nice to me when I have a red ribbon in my hair, and not when I am wearing a blue one? When he cries and I want to comfort him and cuddle him in my lap, it just makes him worse.

When he is frustrated, he says, 'The trains are leaving'. If he wants to sit on the swings, he says, 'There are no more oranges'. For days on end he sings 'choo-choo train', but when I take him to the station and show him a dozen trains and ask, 'And what do you see now?' he says, 'Spaghetti with meat balls.'

'Ordinary people cannot understand why a mother allows her child to bang his head against the wall, or that she doesn't punish her child when he turns her bag upside-down in the supermarket trolley', writes M. Akerley (1988), the mother of an autistic boy who has since grown to manhood.

While autism may well be the best-documented and validated childhood psychiatric syndrome (Rutter and Schopler, 1987), there is still an enormous chasm between the theoretical understanding of autism and understanding it in the practice of daily life.

What is the essence of the problem? Put in the simplest of terms, people with autism find it difficult to deal with symbols, just as there are people who have problems with seeing or hearing. Unfortunately, human society depends on symbols, and language is a perfect example of this. Sounds stand for, that is, things symbolize, actions, thoughts and feelings, and people with autism are known to have great difficulty with language. In other ways besides language, too, social interaction depends on the use of symbols, such as nodding, smiling and shaking hands. It is known that people with autism have great difficulty with social communication.

People with autism consequently live in a world they do not understand, or understand only with difficulty, a world in which they are unable to make themselves understood, or again only with difficulty. So it is not surprising that they apparently withdraw from that world and occasionally express their frustration by banging their head against the wall or flying into a temper.

This withdrawal lies at the root of the name which as been given to the syndrome, or set of symptoms. The word autism was coined by Eugen Bleuler (1911) from the Greek autos (= self) to designate a category of egocentric thinking that is typically present in schizophrenia. When Kanner (1943) described 'autistic disturbances of affective contact in young children' — or 'early infantile autism', as he later preferred to call the syndrome — he used the term rather differently, although with a specific reference to schizophrenia which he at first thought was related to infantile autism but later tried to distinguish clearly from Kanner syndrome. Nowadays, when the term autism is used, Kanner syndrome rather than the schizophrenic syndrome is implied. In a way, the use of the term autism for this childhood disorder is misleading, implying as it does a spurious link with schizophrenia and also that 'extreme aloneness' (synonymous with 'autism', according to Kanner) is somehow at the core of the syndrome.

Just as visual or auditory handicaps have a physical, biological and organic basis, the underlying cause of autism is likewise physical, biological and organic. Understanding of this has grown in recent years and this book considers this view.

And just as people who are born with a visual or auditory handicap require education and guidance matched to their specific handicap, people with autism need education and guidance matched to their particular handicap. This education and guidance are very special, because the handicap itself is very special. They are essential, however, if people with autism are to be permitted to lead something resembling a satisfying life. The educational approach to autism has likewise undergone tremendous change in recent years and is considered here.

This therefore, defines the main ingredients of the book which is divided into eight chapters. These fall into three sections: Chapters 1 and 2 discuss autism in general; Chapters 3 to 5 consist of an introduction to the medical grounds of autism; and Chapters 6 to 8 cover the educational approach to autism. The first two chapters give the clearest possible description of what autism entails precisely.

The medical community and the teaching profession, whose life and work are traditionally separated, should find, inform and inspire each other, if people with autism are to be offered in practice what they can currently be offered in theory. The purpose of this book is to contribute to this endeavour.

Chapter 1
Autism as a Syndrome of Hyperrealism

Steven, Sven and the others

Steven is seven years old. When his father opens the door to the lavatory, Steven says, 'Dirty little boy'. Bizarre language? Bad upbringing? From Steven's point of view his comment is not as illogical as it may sound. Several years ago his father was angry when he smelled for the umpteenth time that Steven had, once again, wet himself, or worse. He took him to the toilet, opened the door and said, 'Dirty little boy'. When Steven sees the door to the cellar, he says, 'And now we are going to eat rhubarb jam'. When he sees the hi-fi set, he says, 'Leave it alone, you'll only break it'.

Sven is 20 years old. He gets distressed if he sees a mounted stag's head and goes to the other side of the wall to see where its body has gone.

'I look at people, see how they treat one another. I divide the behaviours up, write them down, give each behaviour a number, learn them by heart and then try to understand them. But the next time I am confronted with the same behaviour, it is different again', so said another adult with autism.

'All my thinking is visual', says another autistic adult, Temple Grandin, 'I do not think quickly because it takes me some time to form a visual image of what I hear, a video. I cannot remember what people tell me, except when I can convert their verbal information into visual images. Most people in the so-called normal world think in words; but thinking in language and words is foreign to me. I think totally in pictures. Visual thinking is rather like replaying different videotapes in the video cassette recorder of my memory. This method is slower than verbal thinking. It takes time to replay the videotape in my imagination.'

In the Christmas edition of the *New Yorker* (1993) Temple Grandin was interviewed by Oliver Sacks. In his article she returns to the theme of video cassettes which she plays back in her memory. She explains that she now has many videos in her brain which help her to understand much of life but, she continues 'Sometimes when I see people engaged in whatever they are doing, I feel like an anthropologist on the planet Mars. Then I don't have a cassette which helps me to understand what they are doing.'

1

All these people tell us much about the phenomenon known as autism. Steven, for example, is not a badly brought up child who uses dirty words. But, several years ago, his father was angry when Steven had soiled himself and as he opened the toilet door he said, 'Dirty little boy'. These words became associated in a rigid manner with the toilet. And in a similar way, other associations between words or sentences are generated. Steven does not really know what words are used for. He sees things and repeats the words he associates with them. He does what he can, confronted by a world that is too difficult for him. He tries to understand; he tries to makes comments; he tries to be social. Steven shows that autism is not synonymous with wishing to withdraw from social interaction, but rather that autism is often a frenetic bid to achieve social contact.

Sven, on the other hand, knows much of reality but fails to understand that such a thing as a representation of reality exists. Unfortunately human society is full of representations of reality, so Sven constantly finds himself forced to lose touch with human society.

The other adult tells us how difficult other people's behaviour can be for those with autism. In this matter he really does the same as Steven in respect to language: he relates certain behaviours to certain situations, in a frantic attempt to understand some of it and consequently to be able to make himself more understandable. But the creativity and inconsistency of human behaviour are too much for him. Fixed patterns are all that he learns

Lastly, Temple Grandin tells us better than anyone else how people with autism have to depend on visual cues. They think in images, not words, and certainly not in concepts. Her story again underlines how much trouble someone with autism has in following human behaviour with its endless variations. Even someone like Temple Grandin soon feels lost, like an anthropologist on Mars.

The last two cases are obviously people with a high intellectual level. It should be mentioned straight away that they are the exception rather than the rule, because most people with autism also have mild to severe mental retardation. It is these more intelligent people who succeed in communicating something from within about the strange handicap called autism.

An apple and an orange

Sensory perceptions have to be 'processed'. This activity takes place at more than one site in the brain. There are even indications that the left and right sides of the brain are specialized in different types of processing. Normally, one is not aware of this because both sides work together in harmony. Sometimes, however, in pathological conditions, the differences become apparent.

A person whose right side of the brain is damaged, for example, can lose all sense of spatial orientation, no longer be able to find his way, but still be able to talk more or less as before. Someone with an injury to the left side of the brain, however, loses quite a lot of the ability of speech, but has no problems with spatial orientation. It has been postulated that the left and right sides of the brain are also specialized in the manner in which they process information: the right side is thought to stand for 'perceptual synthesis', and the left for 'conceptual analysis'. (Gazanniga, 1970; Rourke et al., 1983; Crawford, 1992).

Take, for example, an orange and an apple, they look alike. For the right side of the brain they look alike because they are both 'round'. Are you rereading that? The right side of the brain immediately 'sees' that they are round. That is why this side of the brain is called the immediate perceptual synthesis. The information 'speaks for itself and no analysis is involved. The round (visuospatial) characteristic is stored in the memory by the right side of the brain quite literally and without processing. For the left side of the brain they look alike because they are both 'fruit'. The conceptual analysis. The fact that they are fruit is not something that can be immediately perceived as such. The left side of the brain helps us to 'go further than the literal' and helps us to organize our observations according to 'abstract' characteristics.

The left side of the brain is also probably specialized in the coding of information into two types of classification:

1. according to abstractions
2. in the order in which it is received.

People with autism tend (at different levels of intelligence) to process information too much in the manner used by the right side of the brain, and not enough in the manner adopted by the left side of the brain. It is this tendency to perceptual synthesis which is partly responsible for their uneven learning profile (Fay and Schuler, 1980; Prizant, 1984; Prizant and Schuler, 1987). At various levels of intelligence, people with autism are less capable of adopting an abstract attitude towards reality. A person with autism is less capable than his intellectual age leads one to presume of going 'further than the information', of going beyond the literal.

Mistähänpitääeniten

Steven's use of language ('Dirty little boy', 'And now we are going to eat rhubarb jam', 'Leave it alone, you'll only break it') is called delayed echolalia. Steven echoes, repeats literally, because this is easier than analysing words in order to ascertain their true meaning. At one time it was customary to frown on this echoing behaviour. It was regarded as too bizarre. Yet echolalia is a commonly occurring phenomenon in normal development: language is imitated before it is understood and used expressively.

Language is imperceptible, abstract. Fifty per cent of people with autism are able to speak, but they use a vast amount of strategies from the right side of the brain for processing auditory information. Echolalia is the speech of the right side of the brain: language is not sufficiently analysed with regard to meaning and is stored in a relatively uncoded manner in the memory, from where it can be reproduced. This is not uncommon. Normal children who are learning to speak sometimes do that as well: they repeat whole sentences or snippets of conversation without really understanding them, but in that way they participate in social interaction.

When we learn a foreign language in the country in question (without educational aids) we likewise have to rely on a similar 'survival strategy'. (I ask for 'Mistähänpitääeniten' and a little while later the video is switched on. The next day, the same request: 'Mistähänpitääeniten' gives the same result: a video film is shown. The day after that I am bored. Again, I would like to watch a video and for want of other words I say: 'Mistähänpitääeniten'. My companions look at me with a smile, but it works, I get a new film to watch. I still don't know that 'Mistähänpitääeniten' really consists of different words, namely: Mistä hän pitää eniten'. My Finnish companions were really asking themselves 'what does he like most?' I was unable to analyse the words sufficiently as regards their meaning, but for want of other strategies I repeated the words literally — my Finnish is very echolalic in character'.)

Frequently, therefore, echolalia is speech which you use to 'survive'; you use the means you have instead of the means others would like you to have. Echolalia is also used as a social strategy — when you wish to converse without knowing how. When you look at it this way, a good understanding of echolalia helps us to appreciate that the old cliché used in connection with autistic people (that it is thought to be related to a lack of motivation) is totally incorrect. Echolalia is a communicative style, *en route* to a more correct form of linguistics. Considered in this light, echolalia is therefore not an element of language which has to be 'eliminated', as was once thought, but a form of speech with a bridging function.

Echolalia is presented here as though it were a relatively simple phenomenon, whereas there are of course many variants.

1 There is immediate echolalia, for example, the immediate repetition of what a person has just said.
2 Then there is delayed echolalia which is repetition after a certain period of time has elapsed. Whereas immediate echolalia is a reaction to the speech of someone else, in delayed echolalia the initiative is taken by the echo speaker.
3 Some echolalic expressions are really literal repetitions, but sometimes slight adjustments are made. For example, 'Do you want to go home?' can become 'Does Tom want to go home?', whereas what is really meant is 'I want to go home'.

4   There are, moreover, enormous differences, measured in terms of communicative intent.

The most primitive form of echolalia is purely reflex-like — a word or a sound like that of a frightened animal. In this form of echolalia, subcortical structures are primarily involved. There are intermediate forms in which the same expression is constantly associated with the selfsame person or situation. When Tom sees his grandfather he always says, 'Pat-a-cake!'. Here one can already suspect a communicative function, but it still has to be deduced by the person who is being addressed. Does Tom really want his grandfather to play the same game with him again? Or is it merely a little phrase which he associates with his grandfather? Is 'Pat-a-cake!' something like the name of his grandfather? When an autistic child approaches an adult, looks at him and says, 'Here's a sweet for you', then the communicative intent (and straight-away the involvement of the left side of the brain, the 'meaning' brain) is immediately a whole lot clearer.

Normal children also repeat almost literally words and short sentences in order to feel 'together' (bonding: Mum, Dad and me). Frequently, the literal repetition also causes them to 'steer' their behaviour, but from the moment they learn how language is put together, they start to use it in a more creative individual manner. This also works much more efficiently. In children with autism, however, this 'own language' develops much later. Meanwhile, their ability to articulate continues to develop, and, in the meantime, their literal memory also continues to develop. The time then comes when they can repeat much longer sentences and combinations of sentences — which also call for greater articulatory skills than those which normal children in their echolalic phase are capable of.

As you see, people with autism frequently say more than they really understand. And, also, the linguistic usage of people with autism is not that abnormal. It is simply that autistic people do not get past the stage of echolalia, or, if they do, only with difficulty.

The hyperrealists

There was the story of Sven, who gets distressed if he sees a mounted stag's head, and there is the story of Johan, a 24-year-old autistic who still panics when he sees a figure of Christ with a crown of thorns. They both fail to understand that this is a meta-reality, a reality behind the true one; it is 'make-believe'.

In play development, by the age of 18 months normal children have already attained a considerable 'symbolic level'. They pretend to drink, and pretend to talk on a toy telephone. What they are creating is a separate world, a fantasy world which runs parallel with the ordinary world. In that fictitious world the child is the actor.

At 24 months this make-believe play is even further removed from reality: that doll pretends it is a human being and this doll pretends that it is drinking... A person with an extremely literal mental set (who believes that the world is what he himself is) is perplexed by this: a surrealistic game is being played here, only he does not know that this is a symbolized reality in a new dimension, a mock reality.

People with autism do not reach the stage of playing with a meta-reality, or if they do, then only with extreme difficulty. They are and they remain hyperrealists.

At the mental age of 18–24 months, children with autism are still discovering reality in a much simpler way. They seek, for example, visual or auditory effects by lining up objects in a row, or by tapping the same alarm clock or sunglasses for hours on end, or they turn the wheels on toys incessantly in the same way. Normal children seek similar effects by way of play at a much earlier age.

The adult world is full of representations, deceptive images and mock realities. Take, for example, the simple word:

BOOK

It has nothing whatsoever to do with what it represents, a book. It doesn't even have anything to do with the sounds of the spoken word 'book'. One might just as well have invented a different and perhaps better symbol. That in fact was done by two artists, Rombouts and Droste, who devised a new alphabet: AZART, which stands for 'Art from A to Z. Each letter was given a — meaningful — graphic representation and at the same time a — meaningful — colour. According to their alphabet, the word 'book' is written as shown in Figure 1.

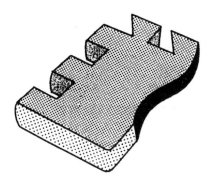

Figure 1.

Suddenly, it is incomprehensible to us. Suddenly, we are suffering from a mild degree of autism because we do not understand the symbols used People with autism understand symbols only with great difficulty. Another example is shown in Figure 2.

Figure 2.

Is this a car? Yes, we say spontaneously. But *is* it really a car? No, but still... The real one is still parked outside. In the real one I shall be driving off later. It is important for us to realize that seeing a connection between a toy car and a *real* car does require a cognitive effort of 'decoupling'. Just as a doll is a symbol for a human being, a toy car is a symbol for a real one. You must be able to see the relationship and understand it.

In recent years a new generation of British researchers has indicated that autism is to a considerable extent a problem of understanding 'metarepresentations' (Leslie, 1987; Frith, 1989). Better-functioning autistic people understand, for example, that the reality is represented by language, but they have extreme difficulty understanding that language should not always be taken literally (there is reality represented in the language — but behind that language a different world can be concealed, a world of 'metarepresentation' which plays tricks on literal meanings, such as irony, hidden meanings, lies... For example: 'My, but you are looking well!'). To pretend, you must of course also have the talent to transcend the literal. People with autism can be said to have a hyperrealistic mental set, and the fact that we do not use words 'correctly' must, to them, seem extremely surrealistic.

What it really amounts to is a lack of imagination. In the most rudimentary meaning of the word, imagination means transcending the literal, adding meaning to observations. People with autism have great problems primarily in those areas requiring the most addition of meaning, namely in the development of communication, social behaviour and play/leisure activities. In these areas their handicap becomes most apparent and they resort primarily to stereotyped and limited patterns of behaviour that they have learned by heart. People with autism therefore have problems with imagination. A person with autism has difficulty understanding the meaning behind the physically perceptible reality. A person with autism has problems with the metaphysical dimension of reality.

A person with autism is a hyperrealist in a world of surrealists.

Chapter 2
Autism as a Developmental Disorder

The significant developmental scales

The history of the scientific study of autism has undergone a focal U-turn in the past 20 years. Initially (in the period when autism was still regarded as a psychosis), the orientation was strongly towards psychopathology. The strange, bizarre, chaotic aspects of people with autism came in for undue emphasis. Titles of earlier books on autism illustrate this; for example, The Empty Fortress by Bettelheim (1967). But people are afraid of things that are 'different' and not understood, and this type of attitude automatically leads to segregation.

Subsequently, the emphasis increasingly shifted to the view that people with autism certainly had a number of special problems, but that much of their behaviour could nonetheless be understood by situating it on the normal developmental scales. The orientation now leaned more towards the developmental view (the international classification systems were also revised, and now regarded autism as a developmental disorder and no longer as a mental illness): the starting point became the comparison with the development of normal children (Schopler and Reichler, 1979; Schopler, Reichler, and Lansing, 1980; Peeters, 1984).

A further observation which should be made at this juncture is that all profoundly mentally retarded individuals will, for example, have difficulty understanding the meaning of pictures and objects. They must not, however, immediately be termed autistic. The great difference is that people with autism are unable to cope with the symbolic level appropriate to their intellectual age. Or, in other words, it is normal at 16 months that words are not yet understood; at 8 months that pictures are not yet understood; and at 4 months that the symbolic meaning of objects is not yet understood. A person with autism, however, has a very different developmental profile and as a result of that a more 'schismatic' personality ('schizophrenia', split personality, one might say, were it not that these terms are reserved for a totally different psychiatric syndrome). And it is precisely in the triad of communication, social interaction and imagination that this schism finds its most striking expression.

9

People with autism are therefore 'retarded' in certain areas. Table 1 demonstrates this in an orderly and understandable manner, by placing the three skills mentioned above alongside the normal development of these skills.

Table 1: Aspects of normal development and early development in autism

Age (in months)	Normal development	Early development in autism
Language and communication		
2	Cooing, vocalic sounds	
6	Vocal 'conversations' or turntaking in face-to-face position with parent Consonant sounds emerging	Crying is difficult to interpret
8	Varies intonation in babbling including questioning intonation Repetitive syllable babbling (ba-ba-ba, ma-ma-ma) Pointing gesture emerging	Limited or unusual babbling (e.g. squeals or screeches) No imitation of sounds, gestures, expressions
12	First words emerging Use of jargon with sentence-like intonation Language most frequently used for commenting on environment Vocal play Uses gestures plus vocalizations to get attention, show objects and make requests	First words may appear, but often not used meaningfully Frequent loud crying, remains difficult to interpret
18	3- to 50-word vocabulary Beginning to put two words together Overextension of word meanings (e.g. 'daddy' refers to all men) Uses language to comment, request objects and actions, and get attention Also pulls people to get and direct attention May 'echo' or imitate frequently	
24	3–5 words combined at times ('telegraphic' speech) Asks simple questions (e.g. 'Where Daddy?' 'Go bye-bye?') Uses 'this' accompanied by pointing gestures	Fewer than 15 words Usually, words appear, then drop out Gestures do not develop; few point to objects

Table 1: (contd)

Age (in months)	Normal development	Early development in autism
	Calls self by name rather than 'I' May briefly reverse pronouns Cannot sustain topic of conversation Language focuses on here and now	
36	Vocabulary of about 1000 words Most grammatical morphemes (plural, past tense, prepositions, etc) used appropriately Echoing infrequent by this age Language increasingly used to talk about 'there-and-then' Much questioning, often more to continue interaction than to seek information	Word combinations rare May echo phrases, but no creative language use Odd rhythm, tone or stress Poor articulation in about half of speaking children Half or more are without meaningful speech Takes parent by hand and leads to object, goes to customary location and waits to be given object
48	Complex sentence structures used Able to sustain topic of conversation and add new information Will ask others to clarify utterances Adjusts quality of language depending on listener (e.g. simplifies language to 2-year-old	A few combine two to three words creatively Echolalia persists; may be used communicatively Mimics TV commercials Makes requests
60	More appropriate use of complex structures Generally mature grammatical structures Ability to judge sentences as grammatical/ungrammatical and make corrections Developing understanding of jokes and sarcasm, recognition of verbal ambiguities Increasing ability to adjust language according to listener's perspective and role	No understanding or expression of abstract concepts (time) Cannot carry on a conversation Virtually no correct use of pronouns Echolalia remains Rarely asks questions; if they do occur, they tend to be repetitive Abnormal pitch and rhythm persist

Social interaction

2	Turns head and eyes to locate sound Social smile	
6	Reaches in anticipation of being picked up	Less active and demanding than non-handicapped infant

(contd)

Table 1: (contd)

Age (in months)	Normal development	Early development in autism
	Repeats actions when imitated by adult	Minority are extremely irritable Poor eye contact No anticipatory social responses
8	Differentiates parents from strangers 'Give and take' object exchange games with adults Peek-a-boo and similar games with a script Shows objects to adults Waves bye-bye Cries and/or crawls after mother when she leaves the room	Difficult to soothe when upset About one-third are extremely withdrawn and may actively reject interaction About one-third accept attention but initiate little
12	Initiates games with increasing frequency Agent as well as respondent role in turntaking Increased visual contacting of adults during play with toys	Sociability often decreases as child begins to walk, crawl No separation distress
18	Peer play emerging: showing, offering, taking toys Solitary or parallel play still more typical	
24	Peer play episodes are brief Peer play more likely to revolve around gross motor activity (e.g. chasing games) than sharing of toys	Usually differentiates parents from others, but little affection expressed May give hug, kiss as automatic gesture when asked Indifferent to adults other than parents May develop intense fears Prefers to be alone
36	Learning turntaking and sharing with peers Episodes of sustained co-operative interaction with peers Altercations between peers are frequent Enjoys helping parents with household chores Enjoys showing off to make other laugh Wants to please parents	Failure to accept other children Excessive irritability Failure to understand meaning of punishment

Table 1: (contd)

Age (in months)	Normal development	Early development in autism
48	Negotiates roles with peers in sociodramatic play Has preferred playmates Excludes unwelcome children from play, verbally (and sometimes physically)	Unable to understand rules in peer play
60	More peer- than adult-oriented Intensely interested in forming friendships Quarrelling, name-calling with peers common Able to change role from leader to follower in peer play	More adult- than peer–oriented Frequently becomes more sociable, but interactions remain odd, one-sided

Development of the imagination

Age (in months)	Normal development	Early development in autism
6	Undifferentiated actions on one object at a time	
8	Actions differentiated in terms of characteristics of objects Use of two objects in combination (not socially appropriate use)	Repetitive motor movements may predominate waking activity
12	Socially appropriate actions on objects (functional use of objects) Two or more objects related appropriately	
18	Frequent symbolic acts (pretends to drink, to talk on the toy telephone etc.) Play linked to the child's everyday routine Active role in 'pretend' play	
24	Applies pretend play routines to dolls, stuffed animals, adults (e.g. 'feeds' doll), frequently Pretend actions not limited to own routine (e.g. pretends to iron) Sequences of pretend actions develop (feeds doll, rocks, and puts it to bed) Pretend play triggered by available objects	Little curiosity about or exploration of environment Unusual use of toys — spins, flips, lines up objects

(contd)

Table 1: (contd)

Age (in months)	Normal development	Early development in autism
36	Symbolic play preplanned — announces intention and searches for needed objects Substitutes one object for another Objects treated as agents capable of independent activity (e.g. doll is made to pick up own cup)	Mouthing of objects often persists No symbolic play Continuation of repetitive motor movements (rocking, stares at light, etc.) Many show relative strength in visual/motor manipulations, such as puzzles
48	Sociodramatic play — pretend play with two or more children Use of pantomime to represent needed object (e.g. pretends to pour from absent teapot) Real-life and fantasy themes can sustain role for extended period	Functional use of objects Few acts directed to dolls or others; most involve child as agent Symbolic play, if present, limited to simple, repetitive schemes As more sophisticated play skills develop still spends large amounts of time in less sophisticated activity Many do not combine toys in play
60	Language is important in establishing theme, negotiating roles, and playing out drama	Unable to pantomime No sociodramatic play

Important!
The autistic development scales should not be taken too literally. For one thing, the earliest stages of autism have not yet been fully charted. Secondly, individual variation is substantial. As a result, certain parents will not readily recognize their child on the basis of the above models.

The even more significant stories

There follows a description of some of the most characteristic symptoms encountered in autism and an outline of development in a typical case. It should be emphasized, however, that there may not be any really 'typical' cases in this field; all people with autism are individuals, and differences rather than similarities prevail. Therefore, it is important to use terminology referring to autism as a disorder affecting individuals rather than using terms such as 'autistic children' or (worse) 'autists'. Children, adolescents and adults with autism have or suffer from autism; they are not autistic. 'People with autism' come in as many shapes and sizes as 'people with pneumonia'. They have different races, social circumstances, intellectual levels, personalities and associated disorders. They should not be expected to conform to a highly specific prototype or to benefit from exactly the same kind of interventions, treatment or training. First and foremost they are people. It so happens that they are affected by the same (or similar) disorder but this does not make them blueprints of each other.

All individuals currently diagnosed as suffering from autism have severe symptoms from all the areas in the triad of communication, social, and behavioural impairment/restriction.

Communication impairment

It is often very difficult to separate symptoms of 'social' and 'communication' impairment. It is, in effect, still unclear whether or not these two domains of problems can be discriminated reliably from each other. Nevertheless, problems specifically referring to preverbal and verbal interactions and comprehension along with those that involve gesture, mime and body language are usually inferred when discussing communication problems in autism. Because of the traditional view that autism involves a triad of communicative, social, and behavioural impairment, we shall treat the communication impairment as a separate type of problem. However, we realize that the separation of communicative from social deficiencies may seem artificial to some readers.

The first year

Some children with autism are abnormal in their development of babbling: babbling may be completely absent, monotonous or appear only for noncommunicative purposes. However, many parents of children with autism report that there was nothing abnormal about their child's development in this respect.

Whereas most normal children are interested in sharing the attention of other people at around 8–12 months of age and are happy to participate in reciprocal games such as peek-a-boo, children with autism usually fail to take an interest in such activities. In a majority of cases they do not develop pointing in the first few years of life, at least not pointing with outstretched index finger.

Many parents report that 'he just would not attend when I called his name or tried to make him take an interest in something in other ways'. The child may 'act deaf', although this should not be taken to mean that the child has actively chosen not to respond. Sometimes the child may react very promptly to spoken language, certain sounds and other stimuli. On other occasions those same stimuli appear not to attract the child's attention at all. It is as though there was some kind of 'on-off' phenomenon with nervous system responsivity being either switched on or switched off. Alternatively, the child with autism may not be able automatically to single out important information from background 'noise', unless his attention has been already 'tuned in' to the relevant information.

Some children with autism are hyperactive from the first few months of life, others are extremely hypoactive. The 'communicative style' of these two groups of children with autism are, of course, very different from each other. The hyperactive child may appear to be more 'communicative'. On the other hand, the hypoactive child may be regarded as 'less of a problem' and so may not be perceived as abnormal, even when there are major developmental irregularities.

The preschool years

During the second year of life, most children start using words that can be understood by people outside of the immediate family. It is when the child with autism does not develop speech the way other children do that the parents realize that something may be seriously amiss. Many children with autism do develop five to 10 (sometimes even more) single words (including words for 'strong stimulus' concepts such as 'ambulance', 'fire brigade', 'dog', etc.), use them for a short while, and then cease altogether. This is often a sign that it is not spoken language that is primarily impaired in autism, but the child's ability to speak and to acquire some language skills, but when repeating words over and over again out of context does not lead to any clear progress, he stops saying them because he cannot understand the point of using them any more.

Many children with autism, after this first stage, remain mute. A minority never develop any spoken language at all. About half of all individuals diagnosed as suffering from autism (Asperger syndrome not included) never develop any useful spoken language and are, for all practical purposes, mute.

The other half of the group, after plateauing or just appearing very late in language development in the first few years of life, begin to echo what they hear other people say around age $2\frac{1}{2}$ to 4–6 years of age. Normal children also develop spoken language through stages of echoing. However, they use their echoed language for communicative purposes soon after having started using it as 'pure echolalia'. The great difference between normal children and children with autism is the way in which the latter group persist with their echolalia for months and years. Palilalia is also very common. This term is used to describe the phenomenon of repeating words and sentences over and over again (often, although not always, in a whisper).

Children with autism often reverse personal pronouns, using 'you' for 'I', 'she' for 'he', 'we' for 'you', etc. This is often a consequence of echolalia: mother asks, 'Are you hungry?' and the child responds by saying, 'Are you hungry?'; mother then says, 'Do not say, 'Are you hungry?', say that 'You are hungry' and the child responds by saying, 'You are hungry'!; soon the child knows that this sentence is temporally related to feeling hungry and he will signal hunger by saying, 'You are hungry'.

The basic communication impairment in autism (just as in the field of social impairment) is the lack of reciprocity and the inability truly to understand the meaning of language use, i.e. to communicate information messages from one person (one brain) to another. If you do not know that spoken language is for exchanging information about beliefs, thoughts and feelings, the best you can achieve is to repeat statements, questions (and only those that you know how to respond to) and whole conversations. True comprehension of spoken language is severely impaired, even when the understanding of individual words is not affected.

Many people with autism have excellent understanding of single words (particularly nouns and verbs which describe things and actions which can be seen or heard in the observable world) and yet fail to understand those same words when used in a context. Parents often tell us that we are mistaken in our view that the child has a language problem: 'He understands so much more than you think, in fact he understands everything'. This is both true and not true: the child may have excellent 'rote' knowledge of single words, but may not be able to piece them together and use or understand them in a full sentence. Thus, the child may understand the word *'out'* and the parents believe that he understands the sentence 'Let's go *out* for a walk'; every time they use this sentence, the child runs to the door, making it clear that he wants to go out. However, the child may equally run to the door every time he hears a sentence such as 'We're *out* of milk!' or 'We'll not go *out* today'.

The school years

For those who do develop spoken language, echolalia and palilalia may continue for many years, sometimes for life. However, a considerable proportion of this group develop communicative speech (of varying degree and quality). Spoken language, even in this group, is usually qualitatively different. It tends to be formal, literal and delivered in a monotone with unusual qualities of voice, pitch and volume.

Thus, from ages 7–12 years there are major communicative differences between different children who have been diagnosed as suffering from autism in the preschool period. Even children who functioned at a very similar level around age 3 years may be completely different five to seven years later: one may be mute and almost completely noncommunicative, the other talkative and long-winded. However, the difference in respect of comprehension of spoken language may not be great.

Many people with autism, including those who are mute, are better at decoding written language than they are at understanding spoken language.

Pre-adolescence and adolescence

A minority of people with autism develop in a very positive way during pre-adolescence and adolescence, perhaps particularly as regards language. They may change so much in this respect that it is very difficult to recognize them as the severely handicapped individuals they were a few years earlier.

At the other end of the spectrum, about one in six to one in four of all individuals with autism deteriorate in adolescence. Some of these lose language skills or become less interested in using the language they may still possess. Others again start using echolalia or palilalia as their main mode of 'interaction'.

Adulthood

The description of predominant adult social style in autism given in the next section focuses particularly on the type and degree of social impairment. The group with continued social withdrawal, and males with an active, odd style, are most likely to be those who are also mute. Women who are active but odd, and men and women with autism who are passive and friendly, are much more likely to have some, even considerable, degrees of spoken language.

Social impairments

Most children with autism show social abnormalities from before their first birthday. Only about one in five has a relatively normal social development up until about age 18–24 months.

The first year

In cases of autism, mothers often comment (at the time when the diagnosis of autism is made, usually after the age of 2 years): 'There was something abnormal from the very first months'; 'There was something odd about him, about his gaze, about his behaviour when I tried to feed him'; 'It was not (necessarily) that he avoided or shunned my efforts at contact, but rather that he did not respond or would not adapt when I tried to hold him'; 'When I looked at him he either stared back without a response, without a smile, or seemed to look straight through me or would fixate on some particular point on the ceiling above me'; 'He seemed so contented when left all to himself, but would be disturbed, even start crying, whenever approaches were made by other people'; 'I felt sad because I could not get him to smile back at me'; 'He never seemed to take an interest when I tried to attract his attention to objects or things that were going on at home or out in the street'; 'When I, or anyone else for that matter, wanted to play with him, he merely stared in front of him or looked in another direction or seemed completely bewildered'; 'Sometimes when I happened on him and he did not know I was looking, he would be engaged in some bizarre activity like rocking himself and his bed or flapping his hand in front of his eyes, and then would stop dead when he noticed I was there'; 'I did not notice anything strange about him, except that he was always so mild, so good, we just could not believe our luck seeing what other parents had to go through, he never demanded anything'; 'From the first few days he would scream around the clock, and it seemed he did not need any sleep at all'; 'He hated it when anyone tried to feed him, and we even had to hang a bottle on a rope for him to feed from when he was lying flat on his back in bed so as not to have to make contact with another person's body'.

Towards the end of the first year of life, it is very common for a child later receiving a diagnosis of autism to have been uninterested in peek-a-boo games, to have declined (or been unresponsive to) attempts at shared attention when looking at everyday things in the environment (the kitchen lamp, a bird passing, a car appearing, etc.) and not to have pointed with his index finger outstretched. Very often, when the child wanted something he would come to those he knew, take them by the wrist and lead them to the desired object without looking the other person in the eye.

It is not uncommon for a mother of a child who later receives a diagnosis of autism to have asked repeatedly at the well-baby clinic, 'Is he really all right?'. It is now quite common for mothers to be very well informed about early child development and to be aware of the existence of autism. Thus, a mother may well ask, 'Does he have autism?' Mothers asking about their children's development, and particularly those asking about the social aspects of development, must always be taken very seriously. It is not that all mothers who ask about such things have abnormal children, but in the past, all too often mothers worrying about these matters were frequently dismissed lightly, and often, without good reason. A thorough examination of the child and follow-up over time is always indicated. Without a proper analysis of the issues, to deny the existence of a problem in the child that the mother feels may be there, could add considerably to the burden of having an abnormal child, and may eventually lead to a lack of confidence in 'experts' on the part of parents.

The preschool years

During the second and third years of life it usually becomes obvious that the child with autism is grossly abnormal in his social development. He does not seem to be interested in other people, and particularly not in other children. He may or may not shun them, and may or may not be completely aloof and 'cut off' from the world. He may approach other people, but only to get what he wants. The typical *lack of reciprocity* now stands out as the major problem. He may enjoy body contact, but will not engage in reciprocal, 'give-and-take' games or interactions. Some mildly affected individuals with autism may stand in the middle of a group of children (or just slightly 'off'), and yet may be surrounded by a curious 'aura' of aloneness.

Gaze is often abnormal, it may be staring, avoidant or simply not directed towards the things and goings-on that attract the gaze of other children and adults. It is not generally that children with autism cannot make eye-contact and that they clearly avoid looking at other people (although those who have autism associated with a chromosomal abnormality called the fragile X syndrome usually do). However, their gaze pattern is abnormal and not as 'lively' as seen in normal children. Interacting with a child with autism may feel a bit eerie, and the interactor, although seeing that the child is looking at him, may nevertheless feel that the gaze is overfocused, too distant, 'vacant' or fixed on the interactor's eyelashes, eyebrows or fringe, rather than on a spontaneous, back-and-forth looking at the eyes themselves.

Some children with autism appear to be so confused in the company of their peers that they start screaming or hitting themselves and demanding to be left alone. Others stand in a corner with their back to the other children. However, in most cases the social abnormalities associated with autism are nothing near as severe or obvious as this. It is instead, again, the lack of reciprocity and the inability to empathize with the perspective of the interactor which characterize children with autism. Some may even accept the company of other children without being able to participate in 'real', 'rewarding' social play. Still others pay no attention to the needs of other people and approach them to get what they want, a favourite object, a dish or a place to watch. In the process they, of course, end up provoking children and parents alike and, as a consequence, may be either feared or bullied depending on factors such as physical assertiveness, physical aggression, height and overall 'style'.

During the early preschool years, many children with autism have little interest for interaction, 'contact' or 'play'. However, a few years later, these same children may be more curious about the environment and may even have developed a, sometimes strong, bond with their parents and siblings, appreciating their presence, perhaps even relying on them to an unusual degree.

There is a widespread misconception that people with autism dislike body contact. Even though a minority withdraw from body contact for most of their lives, the majority really enjoy such interaction, although often only if contact is of the 'rough-and-tumble' type or involves tickling, bouncing, clapping or some such 'hard', 'obvious' or 'rhythmic' interaction. It is not rare for a child with autism to have decreased pain sensitivity, leading to failure to regulate behaviours (including self-destructive behaviour) which may cause physical harm.

The school years

Many, even those who were most detached and distant in the preschool period, develop in a positive way from the social point of view, so that at school age the appearance may no longer be of a child with extreme social abnormalities. He may better accept approaches made by other people and may no longer avoid social interactions. Some may even clearly enjoy having other people around. However, the basic failure to reciprocate is unchanged in most instances.

Except in cases with disintegrative problems and when the underlying causes involve deteriorating brain disorder, positive social development is to be expected in children with autism during this period of life. Failure to progress substantially in the social domain during these years should prompt in-depth re-evaluation of the neurobiological and psychosocial/educational background.

Pre-adolescence and adolescence

Some individuals with autism progress in their social development throughout adolescence into adulthood. A minority take a major leap forward during adolescence and 'emerge' after puberty as considerably better-functioning (relative to age peers) than during the early years of life.

A relatively large group of individuals on the autism spectrum go through adolescence with no major turmoil and without unexpected gains in social development. Unfortunately, a large minority of people with autism (about 40% according to some studies) develop major problems in adolescence. Aggravation of symptoms, with a return of the problems that characterized the earliest years, is common. Severe deterioration also occurs (in about one-third to half of the cases who show some degree of aggravation of symptoms). Some, who developed in a very positive way throughout the early school years, reach a plateau around age 12–14 years and then begin to regress to the preschool level of social development, with more withdrawal, autistic stand-offishness and rejection of other people. Some even lose skills, perhaps particularly some self-help skills. A small number even lose language skills acquired with difficulty in the pre-adolescent period. A sharp increase in problems such as hypoactivity, self-destructive behaviours and stereotypies, is common.

Adult life

By early adult life, the individual with autism has usually developed a personal style which falls into one of the following three categories: 1. continued aloof-autistic, 2. active but odd, or 3. passive and friendly. These styles, reflecting their main mode of social 'interaction', have often been present from much earlier in their lives, but it is only in adulthood that the pattern is sufficiently obvious to warrant clear distinction along these lines. The first group continues to be withdrawn, often refusing to leave their room, or actively avoiding other people. The second group makes one-sided approaches for contact with other people. They may physically touch other people in ways which are socially unacceptable. They are generally perceived as 'difficult', and the active approach is often not appreciated. The third group passively accepts the company of other people and may be perceived by people around them as 'clearly non-autistic'. However, if there is a change of routine or an increase in the degree of social or academic stress, a return to the core symptoms of autism may very well occur.

Behaviour and imagination impairment

Individuals with autism all show abnormalities of behaviour from the first years of life. These behavioural peculiarities are believed to reflect an impoverished, restricted imagination, allowing the demonstration of only a limited behavioural repertoire. In the 'old days' (for instance in Kanner's early writings) it was generally surmised that children with autism had a 'rich inner world' with imaginative abilities sometimes surpassing those of highly intelligent normal children. It is only in the last two decades that it has become generally accepted that individuals with autism are severely restricted in their imagination. This is not to say that they lack all imaginative skills. However, even those few who demonstrate a 'vivid' imagination in some areas usually do so only in an extremely limited field (green monsters, Captain Nemo, Donald Duck, Shakespeare's most famous tragedies, etc.)

Stereotypies and stereotypic behaviour

Many children with typical and severe autism develop motor stereotypies before their first birthday. A motor stereotypy is a repetitive movement of one or several portions of the body. It may be similar to a tic and, indeed, sometimes impossible to distinguish from a tic. A tic is a (usually involuntary) compulsive, spasmodic, often rhythmic contraction of a muscle or group of muscles which is only partially under volitional control.

The most typical stereotypy seen in very young children with autism is hand-waving, hand-twirling or hand-flapping. It is not uncommon for an infant who later receives a diagnosis of autism to have been nicknamed 'The hand'! One of the hands may be held, fingers extended, close to the child's face in front of one of the eyes. The hand may then be rotated back and forth and the child may be watching through his fingers, as if interesting light phenomena were produced that attracted the child's attention.

The most common variants of motor stereotypies seen in autism include symmetrical hand-flapping with both hands, elbows in maximal flexion, finger-flicking (one or both hand), body rocking, head shaking or rotating, and clapping of various kinds. Stereotypic stiffening ('freezing') of the whole or parts of the body and walking high on tiptoe as though in a 'speeded' state are also very common repetitive behaviours which may or may not occur in conjunction with excitement or overstimulation. Some stereotypic behaviours develop into self-destructive activities, such as face-hitting, eye-poking, head-crashing, wrist-biting and thigh-slapping. Given the often reduced pain sensitivity experienced by many individuals with autism, such self-destructive behaviours often become chronic.

Some individuals with autism show motor stereotypies, particularly during the first few years of life. Others show few or no such behaviours in the first two to four years and then have a period of moderately severe stereotypies for one, two or three years, only to show less pronounced behaviours of this kind at a later age. Mild stereotypies (finger traction, hand or finger tapping) may persist but may not be readily observed in people with autism who realize that other people consider such behaviours to be abnormal. There is also one group of people with autism who have no period of clear motor stereotypies, but who usually display a whole host of other stereotypic activities. Particularly in those who are high-functioning, one may come across a mixture of motor stereotypies which, although not purposeful, are certainly intentional, and tics which are clearly without both purpose or intention.

Some individuals with autism exhibit a variety of vocal/verbal stereotypies which may be very difficult to distinguish from tics. They may repeat a certain sound or word over and over again, or may endlessly ask the same question in a highly stereotyped fashion.

Many people with autism live by strict routines and rituals. They may need to walk in and out of the door to the bathroom 10 times before actually being able to enter, or they may spin themselves several times before agreeing to put on clothes in the morning, or they may demand that their mother stirs some butter in the frying pan every morning before they are able to eat the usual cereal with milk, or they may be unable to settle in their bed upstairs at night unless their mother and father and both brothers are standing by the window in the downstairs living-room, or they may demand always to leave a house through a window rather than a door.

After a few years, stereotypic patterns of interest may emerge. This may be most typically seen in those diagnosed as suffering from Asperger syndrome, but it is common in all disorders on the autism spectrum. The most simple of these interests might be seen in those who collect things, part-objects (pieces of plastic, rubble, sticks, greasy paper, things that can be made to spin, etc.) or names and simple facts for memorizing and listing. More complex interest patterns, some in highly intellectual areas, usually do not crystallize until after the age of four or five years.

Certain visual and auditory aspects of objects appear to hold a particular fascination for people with autism. Things that glitter or make certain sounds may be selected by the child or adult for visual or auditory stimulation. For instance, the waving of a spoon of stainless steel for long periods of time may hold the double attraction of providing both motor and visual (glittering) stimulation.

Overall restriction of the behavioural repertoire

It is not only the quality of the abnormal behaviours, such as motor stereotypies, that is typical of autism but also the reduced quantity of behaviours shown that should prompt consideration of the diagnosis of autism.

Most people with autism, regardless of the level of intellectual functioning, exhibit a very limited repertoire of behaviours and interests. Affected children and adults very often occupy themselves doing the same thing over and over again or for very extended periods of time.

Questions are often raised concerning individuals with autism as to why they are doing something. The reasonable answer is often, 'This is the only thing he is well acquainted with and knows how to do'. This type of explanation is sometimes relevant in the case of individuals with autism who exhibit 'abnormal behaviours', such as spending long hours just lying on their bed, standing in the kitchen, rocking back and forth, or masturbating excessively. If an activity can be found which is meaningful to and possible to carry out for the individual with autism, the 'abnormal activity' may cease or diminish rapidly.

The special story of people with Asperger syndrome

In most people — and especially children — with autism, the late development can plainly be heard, seen and felt. People with autism give a 'retarded' impression, even if their general IQ is not unduly low. Then again, there are some people who can likewise be recognized as having autism but who do not give a mentally retarded impression and in whom the high development of certain part-skills is sometimes even more striking than the deficit in communication, social behaviour and imagination. Their verbal communication, in particular, may be quite reasonable. This type of developmental disorder was described by Hans Asperger, and the syndrome now bears his name.

Among specialists there is considerable discussion about the place occupied by Asperger syndrome in relation to 'classic' autism: is it a rather extreme variant of 'normality', with a somewhat weaker ability for communication and imagination; is it ordinary autism with a higher IQ and greater verbal talent; or is it a separate developmental disorder?

For those who wish to look beyond the superficial manifestation, it shares many characteristics with classic autism.

The social abnormalities encountered in Asperger syndrome are often not as striking as those encountered in low-functioning autism. Egocentricity is the hallmark of the disorder, with little or no desire or ability to interact with age-peers. Socially naïve, overly truthful, and embarrassing remarks made by the child/adult to people not well known to him, are characteristic.

The interest patterns with intense study of or engrossment in subjects which may seem odd for the individual's age or cultural setting, are also typical. One child during the early school years had dead composers as his special interest. This particular interest had so fascinated psychotherapists that they had tried for two years to analyse the content and meaning of this without arriving at a reasonable conclusion. The true interest of this boy lay in his fascination with CDs. He liked to watch them spin in his CD player. Like many other individuals with Asperger syndrome, he wanted a 'complete collection' of CDs. One way to achieve this end was to concentrate on dead composers: if they were dead, at least he could be certain that they would not write another symphony!

Routines and rituals may be at a 'higher level' (and be even more elaborate) than those seen in autism. One 10-year-old boy demanded that his parents take him, his brother and sister in the car every Saturday morning so that he might sit in the back and make notes on his checklist, where he made certain that they had driven by every fountain in the downtown area of his home town.

Language development may be late, or later than in brothers and sisters but, once speech emerges, the tendency is for spoken language to develop very quickly, so that at the age of five or six years it stands out as perfect, formal, pedantic, precocious and overly adult. Often language has been memorized by heart and the child may be an expert in superficial conversation. However, there is considerable deficiency in or complete lack of the ability to take the interlocutor's perspective. Speech pathologists often refer to this type of problem with the term 'semantic pragmatic disorder', meaning that in spite of normal or good expressive language skills, there is nevertheless a failure to use language for communication in practical real-life settings. Voice level may be abnormal (too strong, too husky, too low), speed increased or decreased, and speech is often delivered in a flat monotone.

Apart from these language abnormalities, there are other communication problems in Asperger syndrome. Gaze is generally abnormal, and Asperger emphasized its fixating quality. There is a poverty in the range of facial expressions, gestures and body language used. Some may mistakenly be diagnosed as suffering from depression when what they have is (Asperger syndrome with) limited facial expressivity.

Finally, individuals with Asperger syndrome tend to be motor clumsy. Gross motor, rather than fine motor, movements are affected. There may be difficulty in learning to ride a bicycle, to swim, ski and skate. There may be an impression of severe clumsiness, and this is generally most clearly observed in a social setting with many other people present. Fine motor movements (hand skills) may be considerably better, particularly if the individual with Asperger syndrome is manipulating objects that are associated with his favourite interest.

Outcome

We have addressed the subjects of classic autism and Asperger syndrome. For the sake of completeness, it should also be mentioned that there are other disorders in what is known as the 'autism spectrum'. Such disorders are sometimes referred to as 'autistic-like conditions'.

The crucial question in a developmental disorder is whether the people in question can make up all or part of the lost ground. The overall outcome in autism, Asperger syndrome and other autistic-like conditions, is extremely variable, ranging from very poor to excellent. However, in classic cases of autism, psychosocial outcome is generally very restricted and only about 5% develop enough self-help skills and empathy with the perspectives of other people to be able to lead separate lives. About two-thirds of people diagnosed before school age as suffering from autism are completely dependent on other people for their income and lodging in early adult life. Almost one-third may be able to hold down a 'normal' job or live on their own, although usually not both. The best 5% in some cases may be indistinguishable from normal although on neuropsychological testing, problems may still be evident.

Early IQ level and language competence predict outcome fairly well. In those with IQ levels under 50 (corresponding to less than half the level of normal development) almost all belong with the two-thirds who have the poorest outcome. Those with IQ levels over 70 have a more than 50% chance of being in the best outcome category. The earlier the language development, the better the outcome. Epilepsy (present in one-third of all autism cases, see next chapter) increases the risk that outcome may be poor, but there are many exceptions to this rule. The presence of an associated severe neurological disorder (such as tuberous sclerosis, see next chapter) detracts from the possibility of a good outcome.

Much less is known about outcome in Asperger syndrome. However, it is clear that in some cases it may be excellent, and that good, indeed superior, academic functioning and, albeit more rarely, normal family life may be achieved. It is also clear that many pursue a career as a psychiatric patient and require psychotherapy, pharmacological treatment and long-term rehabilitation. How many are in between these two extremes is still unclear.

In non-Asperger autistic-like conditions, outcome is similar to that seen in classic autism. According to some studies it may be slightly worse, given that severe neurological disorders may be even more commonly associated with this diagnosis than with classic autism. However, in some clinics, autistic-like conditions or pervasive developmental disorders are diagnosed in a much larger group of individuals, including those with normal and high levels of intelligence, and outcome in this subgroup may actually be considerably better than in other disorders on the autism spectrum.

Chapter 3
The Medical Diagnosis of Autism and Disorders of the Autism Spectrum

Autism, or Kanner syndrome

Autism (infantile autism, childhood autism, autistic disorder) is not a single disease entity in the sense that, for instance, a specific metabolic disorder is. Rather, the concept of autism represents a comprehensive diagnosis, much along the same lines as epilepsy and mental retardation. It is the final symptomatic expression of brain dysfunction which can be caused by a variety of insults (see Gillberg and Coleman, 1992, for a review).

All current major diagnostic systems (DSM-IV and ICD-10) agree that for a diagnosis of autism to be made, three major impairments have to be present: restriction of reciprocal social interaction, restriction of reciprocal communication (verbal and nonverbal) and restriction of imagination as reflected in a restricted repertoire of behaviours. These three groups of symptoms, when they occur together, are often referred to simply as 'the triad' (Wing, 1989). Triad symptoms have to be pronounced and cannot be accounted for by general developmental delay only. Nevertheless, such retardation is very common.

We shall go into some detail regarding the diagnostic criteria for autism. This may seem superfluous, but is, in fact, a necessary step in trying to — medically — define autism. Whether or not an individual receives a diagnosis of autism depends to a considerable extent on which of the currently accepted sets of diagnostic criteria the clinician is using.

In order to define neuropsychiatric syndromes, use is often made of the Diagnostic and Statistical Manual (DSM) prepared and updated by the American Psychiatric Association. Currently, the vast majority of clinicians will base their diagnosis on DSM-IV (American Psychiatric Association, 1994) which is the fourth revised edition.

The DSM-IV criteria for autism are shown in Table 2. The definition of the World Health Organization (WHO, 1993) contained in ICD-10 (International Classification of Diseases) is very similar.

27

Table 2: Autism: 'Diagnostic criteria' according to DSM-IV

A. A total of six (or more) items from (1), (2), and (3), with at least two from (1), and one each from (2) and (3):

1. Qualitative impairment in social interaction, as manifested by at least two of the following:

    (a) Marked impairment in the use of multiple nonverbal behaviors such as eye-to-eye gaze, facial expression, body postures and gesture to regulate social interaction.
    (b) Failure to develop peer relationships appropriate to developmental level.
    (c) A lack of spontaneous seeking to share enjoyment, interests, or achievements with other people (e.g. by a lack of showing, bringing or pointing out objects of interest).
    (d) Lack of social or emotional reciprocity.

2. Qualitative impairments in communication as manifested by at least one of the following:

    (a) Delay in, or total lack of, the development of spoken language (not accompanied by an attempt to compensate through alternative modes of communication such as gesture or mime).
    (b) In individuals with adequate speech, marked impairment in the ability to initiate or sustain a conversation with others.
    (c) Stereotyped and repetitive use of language or idiosyncratic language.
    (d) Lack of varied, spontaneous make-believe play or social imitative play appropriate to developmental level.

3. Restricted repetitive and stereotyped patterns of behaviour, interests, and activities, as manifested by at least one of the following:

    (a) Encompassing preoccupation with one or more stereotyped and restricted patterns of interest that is abnormal either in intensity or focus.
    (b) Apparently inflexible adherence to specific, nonfunctional routines or rituals.
    (c) Stereotyped and repetitive motor mannerisms (e.g. hand or finger flapping or twisting, or complex whole-body movements).
    (d) Persistent preoccupation with part of objects.

B. Delays or abnormal functioning in at least one of the following areas, with onset prior to age 3 years:

    (1) Social interaction
    (2) Language as used in social communication
    (3) Symbolic or imaginative play

C. The disturbance is not better accounted for by Rett's Disorder or Childhood Disintegrative Disorder

Table 3: Childhood autism: Diagnostic criteria according to ICD-10

Qualitative impairments in reciprocal social interaction, as manifested by at least two of the following four:

1. Failure adequately to use eye-to-eye gaze, facial expression, body posture and gesture to regulate social interaction.
2. Failure to develop peer relationships that involve a mutual sharing of interests, activities and emotions.
3. Rarely seeking and using other people for comfort and affection at times of stress or distress and/or offering comfort and affection to others when they are showing distress or unhappiness.
4. Lack of spontaneous seeking to share enjoyment, interests, or achievements with other people.
5. Lack of socio-emotional reciprocity as shown by an impaired or deviant response to other people's emotions; or lack of modulation of behaviour according to social context; or a weak integration of social, emotional and communicative behaviours.

Qualitative impairments in communication as manifested by at least one of the following:

1. A delay in, or total lack of, development of spoken language that is not accompanied by an attempt to compensate through the use of gesture or mime as an alternative mode of communication (often preceded by a lack of communicative babbling).
2. Lack of varied spontaneous make-believe or (when younger) social imitative play.
3. Relative failure to initiate or sustain conversational interchange.
4. Stereotyped and repetitive use of language or idiosyncratic use of words or sentences.

Restricted, repetitive and stereotyped patterns of behaviour, interests and activities, as manifested by at least one of the following four:

1. Encompassing preoccupation with stereotyped and restricted patterns of interest.
2. Apparently compulsive adherence to specific, nonfunctional routines or rituals.
3. Stereotyped and repetitive motor mannerisms.
4. Preoccupations with part-objects or nonfunctional elements of play material.

Developmental abnormalities must have been present in the first three years for the diagnosis to be made.

There are certain other symptoms which frequently occur in autism, but these are not regarded as essential for making the diagnosis. However, they do deserve to be mentioned: hyperactivity (particularly in early childhood), hypoactivity (particularly in early childhood and adolescence), auditory hyper- or hyposensitivity and variable reaction to sound and noise (obvious especially during the first two years, but usually present to some degree periodically or permanently well into adult age), hypersensitivity to touch, bizarre eating habits, including the ingestion of non-food substances, self-destructive behaviours, decreased pain sensitivity, aggressive outbursts and mood swings. These symptoms are encountered in at least one-third of all people with the disorder.

Disorders of the autism spectrum

It now seems clear that apart from 'classic' variants of Kanner's specific type of autism, there are also 'spectrum disorders' (such as Asperger syndrome) which share many characteristics with the 'core' syndrome without meeting the full criteria for it. The whole group of autism and autistic-like conditions (Steffenburg and Gillberg, 1986) are sometimes referred to as autism spectrum disorders, autistic continuum, or pervasive developmental disorders (PDD).

There was a time when childhood psychosis and childhood schizophrenia were used as comprehensive rubrics for the whole field of autism and its spectrum disorders. However, childhood schizophrenia is now considered as a separate disorder, extremely rare and separate from autism.

Asperger syndrome

It is only quite recently that a syndrome originally described by Hans Asperger (1944) has attracted widespread attention in child and adult psychiatry (Wing, 1981; Gillberg, 1985, Tantam, 1988; Frith, 1991). It concerns, as already mentioned, people with a normal, good or even superior intellectual level. But there is something wrong, and that something is closely related to the same functions that are defective in classic autism.

Asperger syndrome is diagnosed slightly differently by different systems. The DSM-IV and ICD-10 have almost identical criteria except that DSM-IV requires 'clinically significant impairment in social, occupational or other important areas of functioning', a criterion not mentioned in ICD-10. The two diagnostic manuals both require that early language development be normal and that curiosity about the environment and adaptive skills be unaffected. No abnormalities of communication (verbal or nonverbal) are included among the diagnostic criteria. Asperger syndrome is diagnosed according to the same set of diagnostic criteria that apply to autism, except with regard to abnormalities of communication. However, most clinicians agree that it is so rare for an individual on the autism spectrum to have perfectly normal language development, that inclusion of 'normal language development' as a criterion for diagnosis does not make clinical sense. One study has shown convincingly that Asperger's own cases did not meet ICD-10 OR DSM IV criteria for Asperger syndrome!

Gillberg and Gillberg (1989) published diagnostic criteria for Asperger syndrome which were based on the clinical descriptions of patients provided by Hans Asperger himself. These criteria, originally intended for research, were later elaborated by Gillberg (1991). Based on these criteria, an individual who meets the diagnostic criteria for Asperger syndrome may sometimes also qualify for a diagnosis of autistic disorder, and vice versa. This was intentional in order to provide opportunities for studying the possible overlap of so-called high-functioning autism (generally accepted to mean 'autism with an IQ above 70') and Asperger syndrome.

In clinical practice, however, it seems reasonable to add a criterion specifying that Asperger syndrome should not be diagnosed when the full criteria for autistic disorder are met (i.e. the latter diagnosis takes precedence). This has led to the set of criteria shown in Table 4.

Table 4: Diagnostic criteria for Asperger syndrome

Gillberg and Gillberg (1989), Gillberg (1991)

Severe impairment in reciprocal social interaction, as manifested by at least two of the following four:

- Inability to interact with peers in a normal, reciprocal fashion.
- Lack of desire to interact with peers.
- Lack of appreciation of social cues.
- Socially and emotionally inappropriate behaviour.

All-absorbing narrow interest, as manifested by at least one of the following three:

- Exclusion of other activities.
- Repetitive adherence.
- More rote than meaning.

Imposition of routines and interests, as manifested by at least one of the following two:

- Imposition on self, in aspects of life.
- Imposition on others.

Speech and language problems, as manifested by at least three of the following five:

- Delayed development of language.
- Superficially perfect expressive language.
- Formal, pedantic language.
- Odd prosody, peculiar voice characteristics.
- Impairment of comprehension, including misinterpretations of literal/implied meanings.

Nonverbal communication problems, as manifested by at least one of the following five:

- Limited use of gestures.
- Clumsy/gauche body language.
- Limited facial expression.
- Inappropriate expression.
- Peculiar, stiff gaze.

Motor clumsiness, as documented by poor performance on neurodevelopmental examination.

(contd)

Table 4: (contd)

Szatmari et al. (1989)

Solitary, as manifested by at least two of the following four:

- No close friends.
- Avoids others.
- No interest in making friends.
- A loner.

Impaired social interaction, as manifested by at least one of the following five:

- Approaches others only to have own needs met.
- A clumsy social approach.
- One-sided responses to peers.
- Difficulty sensing feelings of others.
- Detached from feelings of others.

Impaired nonverbal communication, as manifested by at least one of the following seven:

- Limited facial expression.
- Unable to read emotion from facial expressions of child.
- Unable to give messages with eyes.
- Does not look at others.
- Does not use hands to express oneself.
- Gestures are large and clumsy.
- Comes too close to others.

Odd speech, as manifested by at least two of the following six:

- Abnormalities in inflection.
- Talks to much.
- Talks too little.
- Lack of cohesion to conversation.
- Idiosyncratic use of words.
- Repetitive patterns of speech.

Does not meet criteria for autistic disorder.

ICD-10 (WHO, 1993)

A lack of any clinically significant general delay in spoken or receptive language or cognitive development. Diagnosis requires that single words should have developed by 2 years of age or earlier and that communicative phrases be used by 3 years of age or earlier.

Self-help skills, adaptive behaviour and curiosity about the environment during the first three years should be at a level consistent with normal intellectual development.

Motor milestones may be somewhat delayed and motor clumsiness is usual (although not a necessary feature). Isolated special skills, often related to abnormal preoccupations, are common, but are not required for diagnosis.

Table 4: (contd)

Qualitative impairment in reciprocal social interaction (criteria as for autism).

Restricted, repetitive, and stereotyped patterns of behaviour, interests and activities (criteria as for autism).

DSM-IV (APA)

A. Qualitative impairment in social interaction, as manifested by at least two of the following:

1. Marked impairment in the use of multiple nonverbal behaviours such as eye-to-eye gaze, facial expression, body postures, and gestures to regulate social interaction.
2. Failure to develop peer relationships appropriate to developmental level.
3. A lack of spontaneous seeking to share enjoyment, interests, or achievements with other people (e.g. by lack of showing, bringing, or pointing out objects of interest to other people)
4. Lack of social or emotional reciprocity.

B. Restricted repetitive and stereotyped patterns of behaviour, interests, and activities, as manifested by a least one of the following:

1. Encompassing preoccupation with one or more stereotyped and restricted patterns of interest that is abnormal either in intensity or focus.
2. Apparently inflexible adherence to specific, nonfunctional routines or rituals.
3. Stereotyped and repetitive motor mannerisms (e.g. hand or finger flapping or twisting, or complex whole-body movements).
4. Persistent preoccupation with parts of objects.

C. The disturbance causes clinically significant impairment in social, occupational, or other important areas of functioning.

D. There is no clinically significant impairment in social, occupational, or other important areas of functioning.

E. There is no clinically significant delay in cognitive development or in the development of age-appropriate self-help skills, adaptive behaviour (other than in social interaction), and curiosity about the environment in childhood.

F. Criteria are not met for another specific pervasive developmental disorder or schizophrenia.

Asperger syndrome and autistic disorder (the high-functioning variant) show an overlap. It is unclear whether or not they represent different places on an autistic continuum. Two interesting models have been postulated to explain the connection between autism and Asperger syndrome, on the basis of empathy and IQ.

It has been suggested that empathy may be a functional ability, conceptually similar to IQ and with strong constitutional roots. According to this model there is a wide variation of empathy abilities in the general population. Only when an individual falls very much below the mean level do we consider making a diagnosis along the autism spectrum. In those with extremely low levels of empathy, autism may be diagnosed and in those with very low, but slightly higher levels, Asperger syndrome may be diagnosed instead.

According to the other model, the only thing that differentiates autism from Asperger syndrome is overall IQ (or verbal IQ). Low IQ (poor verbal abilities) leads to a diagnosis of autism, and higher IQ (better verbal abilities) leads to a diagnosis of Asperger syndrome in individuals who are basically affected by the same type and degree of social impairment. These two models for the relationship between autism and Asperger syndrome need not be mutually exclusive.

Once considered, the diagnosis of Asperger syndrome is not generally a difficult one. The problem is that it is often not taken into consideration.

Childhood disintegrative disorder

There are a small number of individuals who develop normally (or almost normally) for a period of $1\frac{1}{2}$ to 4 years and then develop severe autistic-type symptomatology. Some of these are classified as suffering from 'late onset autism' (usually meaning that there was seemingly normal development up until about 18–24 months). Those with a longer period of normal development followed by plateauing, sometimes frank regression of skills, and development of many of the symptoms characteristic of autism, are often referred to as suffering from 'childhood disintegrative disorder'. In the DSM-IV and the ICD-10 classifications, clinically significant loss of acquired skills (in at least two of the areas: language, play, social skills, motor skills and bowel/bladder control) is required for diagnosis, along with impairment in at least two of the autism triad areas (or, in the case of ICD-10, two of the four domains comprising the triad plus 'a general loss of interest in objects and in the environment').

Childhood disintegrative disorder was formerly referred to as Heller's psychosis, Helier dementia, or disintegrative psychosis.

Other autistic-like conditions

Disorders comprising some degree of autistic symptomatology, but not meeting the full criteria for autism or Asperger syndrome, are currently a major problem from the diagnostic point of view. There is no general consensus regarding their subtyping or naming.

We would like to suggest that any individual with five or more of the symptoms listed by DSM-IV or ICD-10, but not meeting the full criteria for autism, Asperger syndrome or childhood disintegrative disorder, be diagnosed as suffering from other autistic-like conditions.

Autistic traits

Those individuals showing three or more DSM-IV or ICD-10 autism symptoms, but not meeting the criteria for autism, Asperger syndrome, childhood disintegrative disorder or other autistic-like conditions, may best be diagnosed as having 'autistic traits'.

Many children with attention disorders and severe motor clumsiness (children with so called deficits in attention, motor control and perception (DAMP))have autistic traits (Gillberg, 1983). Also, many individuals with mental retardation who do not meet criteria for autism have other autistic-like conditions or autistic traits (Haracopos and Kelstrup, 1975, Wing and Gould 1979, Gillberg *et al.* 1986, Steffenburg *et al.* 1995).

Summary

An overall view of all the disorders of the autism spectrum, including classic autism, includes classic autism, or Kanner syndrome, Asperger syndrome, childhood disintegrative disorder, other autistic-like conditions and autistic traits.

Differential diagnosis

Mental retardation

Autism (autistic disorder, childhood autism) may be difficult to separate from profound and severe mental retardation in some cases. The difficulties are most pronounced in individuals whose mental age does not exceed that of a normal 18-month-old infant. With overall intellectual retardation, some degree of restriction of social, communicative and imaginative skills has to be allowed (just as all areas of functioning would be expected to be affected). The triad problems have to be obviously disproportionate to the overall level of intellectual functioning.

Deprivation and depression

Some severely deprived children and some severely depressed children show many of the symptoms (particularly social and communicative problems) typical of autism. The major difference here is that, whereas autism will remain relatively unaffected by environmental or pharmacological interventions, deprivation and depression syndromes will show marked amelioration (including full recovery) following such measures.

Schizophrenia

Schizophrenia is an extremely rare disorder in childhood. Unlike autism, it is characterized by hallucinations and bizarre delusions. Such problems are extremely uncommon in autism and are not part of the diagnosis *per se*. There is no evidence that autism increases the risk of developing schizophrenia and it appears to be genetically unrelated to that disorder. However, some children who are later diagnosed as suffering from schizophrenia have, with hindsight, often shown autistic-type characteristics, although usually milder and not of a sufficient degree to lead to the suspicion that the child ever had 'clear' autism.

Specific differential diagnostic problems in Asperger syndrome

Asperger syndrome in adults is probably often (mis)diagnosed as semantic pragmatic disorder, schizotypal disorder, schizoid personality disorder, paranoid personality disorder, atypical depression, borderline conditions and even, occasionally, schizophrenia.

Specific differential diagnostic problems in childhood disintegrative disorder

There is a particular problem separating childhood disintegrative disorder from the syndromes described by Landau-Kleffner and Rett. In Landau-Kleffner syndrome there is usually normal early development (for 2–5 years) followed by loss of speech and onset of seizures or severe seizure activity on the EEG. In Rett syndrome there is commonly seemingly normal development for 6–20 months followed by loss of purposeful hand movements, growth stagnation, and various neurological symptoms, often including epilepsy. In both these syndromes, autistic symptoms are common, but they tend to abate with time.

A constantly recurring difficulty: IQ

The vast majority of those with a diagnosis of 'classic' autism have mental retardation, and about 80% have an IQ under 70. Of those with a higher IQ level, almost all test in the 70–100 range, meaning that the diagnosis of autism is almost never made in an individual with above normal intelligence.

The connection between autism and low intelligence level represents a diagnostic challenge, for the autistic triad threatens to be swamped by the overall picture of metal retardation. As a clinician, one has to recognize that the retardation is clearly more important in terms of communication, social skills and imagination, because this has major consequences for the educational approach.

The vast majority of those with a diagnosis of classic Asperger syndrome are of superior, normal or low-normal intelligence. Individuals with autistic-like conditions not diagnosed with Asperger syndrome span the whole range of IQs from severe mental retardation to superior intelligence.

Some authorities consider Kanner syndrome (classic autism) to be the typical low-IQ variant of the autistic syndrome, and Asperger syndrome to be the typical higher-IQ variant of the same syndrome. According to other authors, it is verbal IQ and vocabulary that separate Asperger from Kanner cases, both being higher when the former diagnosis is made.

True autism can therefore ultimately be seen on the basis of IQ as a continuum, on which the lowest portion is represented by severely profoundly mentally retarded individuals with the triad of social communicative and imaginative restriction (Wing and Gould, 1979), the middle section by Kanner's variant of autism (often with mild to moderate degrees of mental retardation) and the upper section by Asperger syndrome (usually with normal or good, sometimes even superior, intellectual functioning).

'Other autistic-like conditions', on the other hand, referred to in DSM-IV as 'atypical autism', is taken to represent an umbrella concept for all the atypical cases of the autistic syndrome regardless of IQ, or is conceived of as a completely different group of problems, albeit with similar symptomatology.

Neuropsychological testing

Neuropsychological testing and psychological laboratory experiments undertaken with children and adults who have autism or Asperger syndrome have produced a fairly consistent picture that may be interpreted in the light of recent developments in the field of study of empathy, theory of mind, central coherence and executive function. First, let us briefly define the four concepts just referred to.

Empathy is the ability of all normal people to mentalize about the thinking and feeling states of other people (derived from the Greek words *em* and *pathos* which were combined by German doctors in the early years of the 20th century to delineate 'einfühlung'). *Theory of mind* is a closely related concept referring (in humans) to the ability (after a few years of development) to mentalize about other people's mental states ('to have a theory that people have minds'). *Central coherence* is the term used for the drive in normal development to try to piece things together, to look at them as details in a Gestalt that forms a 'whole', in short to make things (that happen) connect. *Executive functions* are those that involve planning, motivation, impulse control and the inner experience of 'time'. Merely through stating the definitions of these concepts, it becomes clear that these functions (or rather dysfunctions of these functions) are all implicated in the syndrome of autism.

Children with autism, as a group, reliably test in the low average or mentally retarded range of intellectual functioning on IQ tests such as the Wechsler Intelligence Scale for Children (WISC). About 80% have IQs under 70, and are said to be 'mentally retarded'. Children diagnosed as suffering from Asperger syndrome usually test in the normal or superior range on such tests. Children with a diagnosis of autism often have lower verbal than nonverbal (or performance) scores, whereas those with Asperger syndrome very often (although by no means invariably) have a reversed pattern in this respect.

Some subtests on the WISC are typically low in young children with autism and its spectrum disorders. Results on Picture Arrangement (the child is required to put a set of drawings depicting human actions into the correct order, i.e. to make them constitute a sort of comic strip with a theme) and Comprehension (the child is asked things like, 'What would you do if you hurt yourself?' and is expected to provide 'commonsense' responses, not just statements to the effect that he or she would 'bleed') are almost always much below average levels on the other subtests. With age, children in the Asperger group often score relatively better on the Comprehension subtest but fall behind on another subtest called Object Assembly (a jigsaw puzzle in which the solution is guided by the overall outline of the object depicted (a car, a face, a horse) and not just by the shape of the pieces). The result on Block Design (a test requiring the child to copy a geometric pattern by aligning cubes in a particular way) is usually superior in autism, but may vary considerably in Asperger syndrome

These results have been taken to mean that children with autism have severe problems conceptualizing the mental states ('minds') of other people and, hence, to have empathy deficits. These problems lead to failure particularly on Picture Arrangement which requires insight into the mental states of the human beings depicted in the various pictures. In children with poor verbal ability, failure on Comprehension would also be predicted in children who have a poorly developed theory of mind, because responses would be expected to be concrete and not take into account the perspectives of other people. This is what we find in autism. With higher verbal ability, the 'correct responses' to the Comprehension subtest questions can be taught and learned by heart by the higher-functioning individual on the autism spectrum. This is what we find in Asperger syndrome as the years go by.

Block Design is a test on which an individual with attention to detail rather than concentrating on the 'whole' would not be at a disadvantage. With Object Assembly, it is the other way around. People with decreased drive for central coherence might do well on the former, but would probably fail on the latter. Thus individuals with autism and its spectrum disorders would be expected to do well on the former and poorly on the latter. This is, generally, what we find. However, in Asperger syndrome, motor clumsiness and visual perceptual problems are sometimes a prominent feature, leading to visuomotor problems in completion of tasks, resulting in relative failure on Block Design.

On other tests, such as the Wisconsin Card Sorting Test, people on the autism spectrum appear to be 'rigid', inflexible' and with poor ability to plan and to conceive of time. Such problems are believed to reflect specific executive function deficits. On this test the psychologist has a 'hidden' rule for the correct sorting of differently coloured cards. All the child learns is whether his solution is 'right' or 'wrong'. Normal children change their strategy fairly soon after having been told that their response is wrong. In Asperger syndrome, this often does not occur and children will continue with incorrect responses, stubbornly claiming that they are right.

Several tests have been designed specifically to address the issue of delayed development of theory of mind in autism. The Smarties test is a good example of such a test. Children are shown a typical Smarties cylinder (a cylindrical box containing brightly coloured sweets, a container well known to almost all children, at least in the UK where the primary research was done) and asked, 'What is in this?' Normal children and speaking children with Down's syndrome and autism all say, 'Smarties', because they know that a box looking like the Smarties box usually contains Smarties. The box is then opened to reveal its contents, a pencil. The box is then closed — with the pencil inside and another person (Peter), who knows nothing of what has occurred, enters the room. The child is asked, 'What will Peter say is in the box?' Normal children and those with Down's syndrome usually say, 'Smarties', because they believe Peter has a separate mind that does not have the same information the child does. Children with autism usually say, 'A pencil', probably because they cannot understand that Peter has a separate mind with a belief that is different from their own.

In summary, the neuropsychological tests that have been performed with individuals (children and adults) with autism and autism spectrum disorders suggest that such individuals have empathy problems (theory of mind deficits), that they attend to detail rather than the whole, that they are inflexible in problem solution and deficient in their concept of time.

The incidence of autism in the population

Autism, in classic form, is a relatively rare disorder, occurring in no more than 0.1 per cent of the general population. It was once believed to be much less prevalent, but several studies over recent years are agreed that about one in 1000 children who survive the first year of life develop the syndrome of autism. Asperger syndrome appears to be considerably more common and has been reported in as many as 3–4 children in 1000. Other autistic-like conditions and autistic traits in people with mental retardation and attention disorder may be about as common as Asperger syndrome.

In summary, it seems that autism and its spectrum disorders are more common than previously estimated. The total rate is 0.6–1.0 per cent of the general population of school-age children. Even though there is some increase in mortality in the severely affected group, rates in adults are likely to be of the same magnitude as those in children.

It means, among other things, that practically every GP is bound to have people with autism or with disorders of its spectrum among his or her patients.

Gender differences

Autism is more common in males than in females. In clinics it is usually reported to be at least three times more common in boys. In population studies the over-representation of males is slightly less marked, indicating that in some female cases the diagnosis is missed. This may be because autism may have a slightly different presentation in females. Girls — with or without autism — may have somewhat better developed language and social skills than boys, and their interest patterns may not be as circumscribed and 'technical' as are often those of boys. This may lead to girls with autism having slightly different symptoms: their language use may be better, their interest patterns (dolls, animals, people, for example) may escape recognition as having the typical 'autism quality'. Some of these girls are described as having 'social deficits and learning problems', some as showing 'pathological demand avoidance' (girls who say 'no' and refuse to co-operate) and others still may be diagnosed as atypical variants of 'selective mutism' (a condition in which the individual speaks in the presence of some people, but is mute or almost mute in the company of others).

Asperger syndrome is also much more common in males. The male: female ratio is in the order of 3–10:1, but it is still too early to conclude whether this reflects the true incidence.

Other autistic-like conditions are almost as prevalent in females as in males. In this group many cases with epilepsy and severe mental retardation are included. This subgroup tends towards an almost equal gender ratio.

In summary, there are many more males than females with autism and its spectrum disorders. However, there may be more females with core autism problems than is currently believed.

Chapter 4
The Biological Basis of Autism

What causes autism is not known, but it is clear that it is the behavioural expression of a neurological disorder. This can be suspected from the frequently associated syndromes. For some patients causal medical disorders or circumstances can be indicated. Certain lesions have also been localized and a number of biochemical deviations have been defined. Attention, therefore should be given to the underlying problems in autism, Asperger syndrome and other autistic-like conditions.

Autism seldom occurs alone

Mental retardation

As mentioned before, 80% of people with classic autism have an IQ under 70 per cent. In the case of Asperger syndrome the IQ is higher, while in people with other autistic-like conditions all IQ levels are evident.

Epilepsy

About one in five to one in six of preschool children with autism have already developed epilepsy during the first few years of life (often either so-called infantile spasms, psychomotor epilepsy (temporal lobe epilepsy or complex-partial seizure epilepsy) or a mixture of various types of seizures). Another 20 per cent develop epilepsy (sometimes of a very benign character) in pre-adolescence or adolescence.

The rate of epilepsy in Asperger syndrome may be marginally higher than in the general population, but it is nowhere near as high as in classic autism. Other autistic-like conditions carry an even higher risk of epilepsy than does typical Kanner autism.

Thus, in adults with autism, about 30–40 per cent have, or have at one time had, epilepsy. The brain dysfunction that causes epilepsy in autism is often located in the temporal lobe(s).

41

Impaired vision

At least one in five of all individuals with autism have considerably reduced vision that requires the use of glasses. However, many who are diagnosed as suffering from visual problems at school age later refuse to wear glasses. Blindness is uncommon in autism, but some groups of congenitally blind children have a very high rate of autism. About two in five of all children with autism have a squint in the preschool period. Some of these 'grow out of' such problems before school age, but many retain abnormal eye movements into adult life. Control of eye movements is often at its most disturbed when the child (or adult) with autism is tired.

The rate of visual problems in Asperger syndrome is not known, but clinical experience would suggest it is at least as high as in autism (which is much higher than in the general population).

Impaired hearing

Hearing is often impaired in autism. About one in four have a considerable degree of hearing impairment and a few are completely deaf.

The majority of individuals with autism have normal hearing in the sense that it is possible to obtain a normal hearing test. However, their 'style' of hearing, or rather of attending to auditory stimuli, is very often unusual or pathological. This may have caused considerable concern in the first few years of life with a suspicion on the part of teachers or others that the child might be deaf. Parents rarely believe this to be the case, having experienced the child's extraordinary ability to identify the unwrapping of a chocolate in another room or the sound of a needle dropping on to a carpet.

Speech impairment

Speech and language are impaired in autism, but not in the same way or for the same reasons as in aphasia or dysphasia. In the latter conditions, the ability to speak is primarily affected. In autism, the primary defect is the individual's reduced capacity to grasp the meaning of communication, namely the sharing of information (knowledge, feelings) between two minds. This ability is usually spared in dysphasia.

In a minority of individuals with autism (about one in five, according to clinical experience), speech itself is hindered and there is concomitant autism and dysphasia. This combination of problems should be suspected in individuals with autism who appear to want to talk but who seem to be unable to do so. These are people who have never talked, unlike those who had a period of some (albeit minimal) speech development. Most people with autism actually have the ability to talk, they just cannot understand the purpose of talking!

Possible causal factors

Medical disorders

About one in four of all individuals diagnosed as suffering from autism have an associated medical disorder with a known or probable cause. The fragile X syndrome and other genetic/chromosomal disorders, including Angelman syndrome, tuberous sclerosis (a genetic, so-called neurocutaneous disorder with a combination of skin and brain problems), Ito's hypomelanosis (also a neurocutaneous disorder with hypopigmented skin areas and brain problems), fetal damage caused by rubella infection *in utero*, or by certain environmental toxins, postnatal herpes encephalitis (infectious inflammation of the brain) and metabolic disorders (including the so-called phenyl ketonuria syndrome) are among the best known of these disorders. It is still not known just what these medical disorders have in common, but it is generally believed that they impair brain functions which are necessary for normal social, communicative and imaginative development. The temporal and frontal lobes of the brain are most often involved when the above mentioned disorders are combined with autism. The association of autism (and autistic-like conditions) with these disorders is important for at least two reasons. Children and pre-adolescents with autism need to be properly worked up from the medical point of view to identify or exclude these (and a list of other, even rarer) conditions. Also, their presence in autism is of great theoretical interest as they may contribute to our understanding of the brain areas or brain systems that need to be dysfunctional for autism to occur.

Heredity

Siblings of children with autism have a much increased risk of having autism. About one in 20 of full siblings of people with autism have autism (compared with one in 1000 in the general population). This is a particularly high risk given that so-called genetic stoppage occurs in autism. Genetic stoppage means that families who have a child with a severe disorder — such as autism — tend to have fewer children than do those who have normal children.

Twin studies have demonstrated convincingly that the rate of autism is much higher in identical than in non-identical twins of individuals with autism. This indicates that there is a strong genetic contribution to the cause of autism. However, it is not known just how large this genetic contribution may be in the individual case, how much of the genetic variance that is accounted for by other genetic medical disorders, or exactly what it is that is inherited. According to some studies, the inherited trait may be some kind of cognitive disability (such as mental retardation or dyslexia). Other studies have indicated the importance of an inheritable social deficit on the autism spectrum, similar or identical to the clinical syndrome described by Hans Asperger. Yet other studies suggest that autism may be the result of specific combinations of 'susceptibility' genes that may cause either mild social impairments, obsessive-compulsive symptoms, language and communication problems or combinations of these in relatives of severely affected individuals. Results from these studies have suggested the existence of a 'broader (or lesser) autism phenotype'.

In Asperger syndrome, at least in clinical groups of patients with this diagnosis, there is often a first-degree relative (father, brother or, more occasionally, mother) with Asperger syndrome or a similar type of personality problem. About half of all individuals diagnosed with Asperger syndrome have a near relative with the diagnosis or obvious symptoms of it.

Early brain damage

More children with autism than in the general population have suffered brain damage in pregnancy, during delivery or in the postnatal period. In particular, they often have reduced optimality in the prenatal and neonatal periods. That is to say, they often had several minor problems in pregnancy and later, abnormal states which, in themselves, would probably not cause harm to the fetus or the newborn baby, but that taken together create a milieu in which the developing brain never has an optimal chance of positive growth.

In Asperger syndrome there is also quite often a history of problems during delivery or in the neonatal period. Abnormal modes of birth may be particularly common in this group.

Children who suffer certain infections, such as rubella in pregnancy or herpes virus infection in the first few years of life, appear to be at much increased risk for the development of autism. Other infections too may cause brain damage necessary and sufficient to produce autism.

Morphological and biochemical signs of brain dysfunction

A great number of studies have shown individuals with autism to have high rates of demonstrable brain dysfunction. Abnormalities can be demonstrated on CAT scan (computed axial tomography, a form of X-ray examination) or MRI scan (magnetic resonance imaging, a non-X-ray form of imaging) of the brain, but they are not consistent from one case to another and there are still many individuals with autism who have no demonstrable brain abnormalities according to these examinations. A subgroup of individuals with autism have abnormalities of the cerebellum and another subgroup have changes in the temporal lobes and around the ventricles.

SPECT findings (single photon emission computed tomography, a method for measuring blood flow and hence nerve activity in the brain) indicate that the temporal lobes (and sometimes the frontal lobes) are dysfunctional in autism. It is possible that the highest functioning autism group (including those with Asperger syndrome) may have more frontal lobe than temporal lobe dysfunction. This is also supported by findings from PET studies (positron emission tomography, another method which measures the brain's functional activity) and from studies in which children with autism and Asperger syndrome have been examined with neuropsychological tests.

Brain stem dysfunction according to auditory brain stem response (ABR) examination occurs in one-third of all individuals with autism. A further one-fifth have other abnormalities suggesting brain stem dysfunction (squints, abnormal eye movements). Together, 50–55 per cent of all individuals with a diagnosis of autism have some evidence of clear brain stem damage or dysfunction.

About one in two of all individuals with autism have clearly abnormal EEGs (electroencephalograms), usually with temporal lobe abnormalities. The rate seems to be high in both high-functioning and low-functioning individuals with the disorder.

Examination of the cerebrospinal fluid (the liquid that surrounds the brain and of which specimens can be obtained through lumbar puncture) reveals several abnormalities. There is often an imbalance of certain neurotransmitters (substances responsible for the transmission of impulses across nerve cell contacts/synapses), in particular a relative increase in dopamine-breakdown products and a decrease of noradrenalin-breakdown products. The levels of glial fibrillary acidic (GFA) proteins secreted by nerve cell supporting tissue (so called astroglial cells) are probably increased, as are levels of certain gangliosides, which are secreted to the cerebrospinal fluid when synapses/nerve cells have broken down. The findings from these types of analyses may help our understanding of the neurochemical processes and nervous system abnormalities which are involved in the development of the clinical syndrome of autism, but they are, as yet, of little or no help in the diagnostic procedure.

Autopsy studies of young individuals with autism who died accidentally have shown abnormalities in the cerebellum, brain stem and temporal lobes (and the amygdala in particular).

In Asperger syndrome, the rate of reported abnormalities in brain functions/brain structures is usually lower than in autism, but higher than in the general population.

Putting one's finger on the problem

The various laboratory brain neurochemistry finding in autism suggest that there may be several variants of brain dysfunction which can lead to the full syndrome of autism. The big head, the autopsy findings and the high levels of GFA protein, gangliosides and dopamine-breakdown products all suggest an over-production of nerve cells with resultant abnormal/dysfunctional synapse formation and breakdown. The nerve cells may be more 'isolated' in the brains of people with autism than in normal brains. The temporal lobes, the brain stem and the cerebellum are affected in many cases, and these areas (interconnected through various neural circuitries) are likely to be of fundamental importance for the development of social and communicative interaction.

1. The *temporal lobes* are crucial for the understanding of spoken language, for semantics and pragmatics and for the fine-tuning of affective states. The amygdala (deep in the temporal lobes) appears to have an especially important role — a switchboard mechanism of sorts — in the co-ordination of social interaction.
2. The *brain stem* is something of a 'mailbox' for incoming sensory stimuli.
3. The *cerebellum* is involved in co-ordinating motor movements, not least in connection with social interaction. It also has some other important functions in the subserving of social interaction.
4. The implication of the involvement of the *frontal lobes*, particularly in the highest-functioning cases (including Asperger syndrome) also seems reasonable. Executive functions (planning, motivation, time concepts, impulse control) are dependent upon the optimal functioning of the frontal lobes. Such functions are often deficient in high-functioning variants of disorders on the autism spectrum.

A provisional synthesis

Autism is the behavioural expression of neurological dysfunction, based on brain abnormality. The causes of these brain problems are multiple. It is clear that some cases of autism are genetic and that others are caused by specific brain problems associated with other specific medical conditions. It is not yet known how large a proportion of all autism cases is caused by one or the other mechanism. It also appears that the syndrome of autism can occur following brain damage incurred in pregnancy, around delivery or, sometimes, in the postnatal period.

Empathy problems (theory of mind deficits/mentalizing problems), decreased drive for central coherence, and executive function deficits may all be mediators between the neurological abnormalities and the behavioural triad of impairments typical of autism and its spectrum disorders. These cognitive or neuropsychological problems may be specifically correlated with dysfunction of certain neural circuitries in the temporal and frontal lobes and in the brain stem cerebellum. Dysfunction of these areas may result in neurochemical abnormalities which can be detected by examining the cerebrospinal fluid of individuals with autism.

Autism is possibly the most severe expression of the disorder, and Asperger syndrome constitutes a milder variant (at least in some cases). One hypothesis proposed that, in some cases, Asperger syndrome may be inherited as a 'personality trait' and autism occurs when brain damage is added to this heritable trait. However, in other instances it appears that autism (or a liability to develop autism) can be inherited without the addition of brain damage. It also seems clear that Asperger syndrome can result from brain damage without the contribution of genetic factors.

Conclusions

All individuals with a diagnosis on the autism spectrum need to be worked up by a team consisting of, at the very least, a medical doctor (neuropsychiatrist, neurologist or developmental paediatrician), a psychologist (with considerable training in neuropsychology and experience in the field of autism) and an educational specialist (with considerable experience in the field of autism)

Children with autism (and non-Asperger autistic-like conditions) under 10 years of age should have neuropsychological tests (IQ level as a minimum), tests of vision and hearing (usually including a test of auditory brain stem responses), chromosomal culture, DNA test to exclude/ diagnose the fragile X syndrome, EEG, neuro-imaging examination (e.g. CAT scan or MRI scan) and blood and urine tests (to exclude certain metabolic disorders). Lumbar puncture, with examination of the cerebrospinal fluid, is performed in many countries, but is felt necessary only in certain instances in other parts of the world.

For young children with Asperger syndrome, the need for work up may be similar/identical to that described for autism. However, if there is a clear family history of the disorder and there are good reasons to assume that a specific medical condition is not the cause of the familial loading, examinations may be limited to neuropsychological tests, tests of vision and hearing, chromosomal culture and DNA test for fragile X.

For older individuals, there is always a need to consider a full medical/neuropsychological workup, but many factors enter into the equation after the age of 10 years. For instance, some of the disorders (tuberous sclerosis, some neurodegenerative disorders, classic Rett syndrome) that are known sometimes to cause autism will have presented with other evidence of its existence around age 10 years, and so a full work up — as described for young children with autism — may not be indicated in this age group.

The family will need genetic counselling, which should be given only after a full medical work-up has been performed.

Chapter 5
Education and Guidance of People with Autism: Medical Viewpoint

Traditionally, medical doctors and teachers belong to separate worlds; doctors to hospitals and clinics, and teachers to schools. The barriers between these worlds are surprisingly strong, and it is rare for neurologists and psychiatrists to work in close collaboration with specialists in the field of education. Autism, Asperger syndrome and other autistic-like conditions are all medical disorders which require the long-term intervention, assistance and education provided by teachers, be they special education teachers or not. The need for close collaboration between 'the medical people' and 'the school people' is obvious in this field.

The need for structure

Chaos

The chaotic inner experience of a child with autism who does not understand that other people have separate minds and that their actions reflect their thoughts, plans and feelings needs to be counteracted by providing a very clear and predictable environment.

The disturbed time concept

One important aspect of structure is time. In essence, there can be no environmental structure without consideration of the concept of time. However, we believe that the failure on the part of individuals with autism spectrum disorders to appreciate the meaning of time (indeed, to have an intuitive feeling of time) is not generally appreciated either by doctors or teachers. We therefore refer to this impairment separately in order that it be dealt with in sufficient depth in school and at home.

Frequent medical problems

Mental retardation

People with autism spectrum disorders have a wide range of intellectual abilities. Some are profoundly retarded with no speech and may have limited ambulation. Others, especially those diagnosed as suffering from Asperger syndrome, have a high IQ, speak in full sentences (and may even be over-talkative) and are very active. It should be obvious that individuals with such different ability levels need to be approached and taught in different ways, even in different settings. For instance, it would not generally be appropriate to have children with autism with profound mental retardation attend the same classroom as a high-functioning individual with Asperger syndrome. The diagnosis of autism must never be used as the only basis for deciding on the best educational setting. People with autism are individuals and they need the same degree of diversification in terms of educational opportunities as do any other children.

Epilepsy

Many people with autism also have epilepsy. Teachers need to be aware that at least one in three of all individuals with classic autism have epilepsy (or have had epilepsy when younger). Those with early onset variants of epilepsy have problems which are usually well known to the parents, who have often informed the teachers in some detail about procedures should a seizure occur in school. However, quite often the first seizure occurs in pre-adolescence and adolescence and the teacher may be the first to see the child have a major or minor convulsion.

Epilepsy may be of the classic *grand mal* type, with major seizures, stiffness and rhythmic contractions in major muscle groups, loss of consciousness and (sometimes) biting of the tongue, respiratory arrest, bluish discolouration and (more rarely) loss of sphincter tone with subsequent loss of urine and faeces control. The seizure may last for several minutes and is often followed by deep sleep. The individual should be placed on a bed or on the floor, on one side (to prevent damage through falling, aspiration or breathing dysfunction through obstruction). Tight-fitting collars should be (gently) loosened. There is usually no need to insert anything in the mouth, and clenched jaws should not be vigorously separated. The seizure often subsides without further intervention, but, if prolonged, may warrant the administration rectally of a muscle relaxant (such as a benzodiazepine), or even transportation of the individual to an emergency room. In most cases of autism with epilepsy, instructions as to how to behave in circumstances brought about by seizures will have been provided by the physician in charge of the anti-epileptic treatment. However, if the first major convulsion appears in school, the teacher may be totally unprepared and frightened. It is important to try to stay calm and, if possible, to check the time of onset of a seizure (in order later to be able to judge how long the whole episode lasted). In the vast majority of all *grand mal* seizures, the episode is self-limiting and convulsions subside within minutes. Unless convulsing continues for a quarter of an hour or more, usually no severe damage will be incurred by the seizure. Nevertheless, at the end of about five minutes it may be prudent to request an ambulance. A teacher should never worry about calling an ambulance or asking for medical assistance. The principle of 'once too often' rather than 'once too late' is appropriate.

Epilepsy may be difficult to diagnose. This is true in a person without autism, and diagnosis is often even more difficult in somebody with autism. Some variants of epilepsy present with predominantly psychiatric/psychological symptoms, including strange behaviours, strange looking/staring spells, automatisms, and spells of absence or withdrawal. Such symptoms may be difficult to separate from core characteristics of autism without epilepsy. Any child with 'absence spells' should be evaluated for the possible presence of epilepsy. A teacher or parent, rather than a psychiatrist or neurologist, may sometimes be a better observer of such symptoms which could signal underlying epilepsy. Keeping track of such symptoms through systematic recording in a notebook is usually very helpful in differential diagnosis. The doctor trying to decide whether a child with autism has an atypical, unusual or just difficult-to-diagnose variant of epilepsy will find such systematic note-taking extremely useful.

Drugs which are used to reduce seizure activity — often referred to as anti-epileptic drugs — sometimes have negative effects on the child's emotional, behavioural and academic functioning (see below). Teacher observations of changes in behaviour and intellectual functioning are helpful for the clinician seeking to adjust dosage of medication to the most appropriate level.

Visual problems — disturbed eye movements

Visual problems are encountered by a relatively large subgroup of people with autism and are rarely dealt with appropriately. Often a child with autism simply refuses to wear glasses. Unfortunately, this behaviour is sometimes accepted without further examination and blamed on the ritualistic tendencies of the child. If a child with autism has a refractory anomaly or another reason for impaired vision, this needs to be dealt with thoughtfully, so that the child can take full advantage of any special aids (glasses, squint training) or operations (usually for constant squints). The importance of the ophthalmologist being well acquainted with children with autism cannot be overemphasized. It is usually very difficult for an ophthalmologist inexperienced in the field to get a child to co-operate well enough to provide a basis for examination which will allow balanced and reasonable recommendations.

If a child with autism has a well-documented need for glasses, he must be strongly encouraged to use them. This may take considerable ingenuity on the part of doctors, parents and teachers, but it is a collaborative effort which is usually well worth the time and commitment invested. It is not unusual to see a child with autism make unexpected academic gains after the successful completion of 'training' in wearing glasses.

Blind children with autism present particular problems, and as a group are one of the biggest challenges in the whole field. Blindness carries a much increased risk of autism, an association which has not been sufficiently explored in the past.

Hearing deficits

At least one in 25 people with autism are deaf or almost deaf, and about one in 10 have a considerable hearing deficit. Hearing-aids may be very useful for those with severe hearing deficits. For some with mild to moderate hearing impairment (less than 35 dB), a hearing-aid can be more of a nuisance than a help. Many people with autism are so disturbed by unusual sounds and noise that a hearing-aid has little to offer them other than an escalation of their hearing problem. As with glasses for those with refractory anomalies, hearing-aids should be fitted by specialists who are well acquainted with the problems associated with autism.

Sign language and other alternative nonverbal modes of communication may be very important for improving the quality of life of some individuals with autism, perhaps particularly when there is an associated hearing deficit.

Specific speech and language problems

The majority of individuals with autism and autistic-like conditions do not suffer from specific problems of speech or language. Only about one in five has such specific problems that cannot be accounted for simply by the impaired understanding of the meaning of communication, which is a hallmark of the autistic syndromes. When an individual with autism has a specific difficulty in producing spoken language (for instance because of impairment of neurons and muscles involved in vocal cord movements), the appropriate term would be dysphasia. Thus, somebody with this combination of problems has both autism and dysphasia. Sign language and other alternative modes of communication should be tried in all such cases. Such measures may sometimes be a complete waste of time in individuals with autism spectrum disorders without dysphasia.

Skin abnormalities

Many of the various medical syndromes that are associated with autism comprise skin problems. In tuberous sclerosis, neurofibromatosis and hypomelanosis of Ito (disorders that between them occur in about 6–10 per cent of all autism cases), small or large areas of skin are hypo-pigmented. In tuberous sclerosis there are additional skin abnormalities, some of which develop only after the preschool period. A brownish-red to purple rash with hard papules extending over the nose and cheeks is common, and may, at least in the early stages, be mistaken for common pimples. In neurofibromatosis there may be skin-coloured nodules (neurofibromas) and papules, a multitude of discoloured skin patches referred to as *café-au-lait* spots and changes in the bones of the skull and other parts of the body. The facial changes in tuberous sclerosis and the neurofibromas in neurofibromatosis are sometimes amenable to surgical treatment. Most other skin changes do not require therapeutic intervention.

Bone and joint problems

Some of the medical syndromes associated with autism (Rett syndrome, marker chromosome 15 syndrome) often lead to abnormalities of the spinal column with skewing of the whole back (scoliosis or kyphosis). This may lead to major problems in remaining seated for long periods of time. From adolescence, the back problems in Rett syndrome are usually so severe as to warrant orthopaedic treatment and a majority of girls with this syndrome are confined to a wheelchair from adolescence.

Individuals with the fragile X syndrome are often hypotonic and have an abnormal degree of ligamental laxity leading to joints that may be 'overflexible'.

Those who have Moebius syndrome often have slight to moderate malformation of the hands and feet. These problems may lead to considerable gross and fine motor clumsiness/dysfunction which may adversely affect optimal functioning in school.

Malformation of external genitalia

Adolescent and adult males with the fragile X syndrome usually have very large external genitalia (the testicles in particular). Those with other chromosomal abnormalities (XXY syndrome, Prader-Willi syndrome) may instead have very small external genitalia. Both types of abnormality may cause considerable cosmetic (and even some major emotional) concern, not least in the physical education setting at school.

Temporal lobe dysfunction

The fact that so many people with autism have temporal lobe abnormalities is important in the school setting for several different reasons. Temporal lobe dysfunction may be responsible for language and comprehension problems in autism. It is also a common trigger of aggressive outbursts and other 'primitive' behaviours. Lastly, the temporal lobes are often the site of epileptogenic discharges leading to various kinds of seizures, fits or absences which interfere with behaviour and normal learning.

Brain stem dysfunction

People who have brain stem dysfunction according to ABR examination (see Chapter 3 on diagnosis) usually have some structural abnormality in the brain stem. This abnormality often leads to prolongation of transmission of impulses through this ('low') region of the brain. Auditory impulses are often delayed by 15–20 per cent or more. This very likely leads to disruption of coding of ordinary (fast) spoken language, which requires fast transmission through the brain stem for effective decoding/comprehension on the part of the 'receiver'.

Thus, individuals with autism who have abnormal results on ABR examination (with prolongation of the brain stem transmission time) may need other people to talk very slowly and to use only a few words at a time in order that they might understand spoken language better.

Further, it has been our experience that people with autism who also have brain stem dysfunction (either according to ABR examination or some other test, such as a test of post-rotatory nystagmus) seem not to tolerate music (or some kinds of music) very well, more often than those who have normal brain stem function. This is important because there is a widespread belief that all people with autism love music. This is certainly not true. ABR examination may sometimes serve as a guide for the identification of those who are likely to suffer most from 'over-exposure' to music. This, of course, is not to say that music may not be very much appreciated by many people with autism and its spectrum disorder.

Many people with autism have moderate hypotonia, i.e. their overall muscular tone is low and they may appear flaccid and clumsy as a result of this. Brain stem dysfunction (and cerebellar dysfunction) may be the underlying cause of such hypotonia.

Cerebellar dysfunction

The findings in several studies that the cerebellum is dysfunctional in many cases of autism spectrum disorders may be linked to the clumsiness which is often present. In the old days, it was generally surmised that autism was somehow associated with excellent motor skills. Systematic study has failed to confirm this, and most individuals with autism have some degree of motor clumsiness. It may be at its most pronounced in Asperger syndrome. The inability to co-ordinate movements of various parts of the body at the same time, the less than perfect fine motor skills, the slightly 'shaky' and unstable gait, and high anxiety encountered in many young children with autism and Asperger syndrome, might all be reflections of abnormal function of the cerebellum. 'Awkward' body language during social interaction may also be caused by cerebellar dysfunction.

Self-destructive behaviour

Many individuals with autism are self-destructive. They hit themselves or bang or crash their heads against walls, floors and windows. People with autism and severe mental retardation exhibit the most problems in this area and they are also the individuals who have the most difficulty in communicating (verbally and nonverbally) with other people. It is always essential to consider the possibility of an underlying physical disorder in such cases, perhaps especially when such symptoms appear for the first time in an individual who has not previously engaged in such activities. A broken bone or jaw, a middle ear infection, pneumonia or appendicitis may all produce pain that the person with autism cannot deal with or communicate about in any other way than by being self-abusive. Occasionally, the ingestion of needles, razor-blades, plants, etc. may cause severe bowel problems which will be signalled only through increased levels of self-destructive behaviours. Thus, a physician must always be consulted when dealing with self-destructive behaviours.

Problems associated with specific syndromes of the autism spectrum

Fragile X syndrome: 'turning-away-on-greeting'

In the fragile X syndrome there is almost always a curious 'turning-away-on-greeting' behaviour and a particular type of 'gaze avoidance'. It is important to take both of these into account when planning education. For instance, the often cited sentence 'it is necessary for a teacher to make eye-contact before education can begin' may not hold true in autism associated with the fragile X syndrome. In our experience, accepting that the child looks the other way, avoids the teacher's gaze and may actually turn his whole body around so that his back faces the teacher, is usually a key to better communication, instruction and teaching. Nervous giggling, hyperactivity, midline hand-clapping, frantic hand-rubbing, wrist or knuckle-biting and a mixture of hyperventilation and sighing are common features of the fragile X syndrome (with or without the full syndrome of autism). Symptoms of severe withdrawal and other major autism symptoms often improve over the years in the fragile X syndrome. The rate of epilepsy appears to be lower than in the 'average autism group'. The degree of mental retardation is generally mild to moderate with IQs mostly in the 30–70 range.

In fragile X syndrome with autism there is often extreme hyperactivity and attention difficulties which add considerably to the overall level of handicap. The overactivity is often most pronounced during the preschool and early school years.

Tuberous sclerosis: staring gaze and irritability

Autism in tuberous sclerosis is often (although by no means always) severe and coupled with marked withdrawal, staring gaze and irritability. Fits of rage and explosive outbursts of hyperactivity and self-destructiveness are common. The rate of epilepsy is exceptionally high in this syndrome. Mental retardation is often severe or profound in these cases. However, children with tuberous sclerosis and autism (or Asperger syndrome) with mild mental retardation, or even average levels of intelligence, have been described.

Rett syndrome: extreme stereotypies and limited hand function

In Rett syndrome, which may sometimes lead to the full syndrome of autism and which probably occurs in girls only, there is typical hyperventilation, teeth grinding, refusal or loss of hand use, muteness, midline hand-clapping, hand washing or other kinds of stereotypies and odd laughing spells, in combination with typical physical problems including epilepsy, ataxia, stunted growth, coldness of hands and feet and scoliosis. Almost all cases are profoundly mentally retarded, but 'higher-functioning' variants of Rett syndrome (even some with some preserved speech) have been described. The majority of girls/women with Rett syndrome have no or very limited active use of their hands. The 'compulsive' repetitive hand-washing and other kinds of hand stereotypies interfere with almost all activities, including the training of what little constructive hand function may be present. Fixing one of the hands may improve the chances of training functions in the other hand.

Partial tetrasomy 15 syndrome: hyperventilation and hyperacusis

In the partial tetrasomy 15 syndrome (marker chromosome 15) there is often hyperventilation, hyperactivity and hyperacusis (exaggerated reaction to sound or to certain sounds). Epilepsy is more common than in other autism cases and the overall level of retardation is mostly moderate, severe or profound.

Moebius syndrome: facial immobility

Some children with autism have Moebius syndrome with bilateral (sometimes partial, sometimes total) paralysis of the facial nerve with partial or complete immobility of the facial muscles. Such individuals may appear to be depressed because of their absence of facial expression. They often have difficulty in chewing and swallowing, symptoms which are generally common enough in autism but which are worse in this syndrome because of neuromuscular dysfunction. The level of intellectual functioning in Moebius syndrome with autism is from low normal intelligence to profound mental retardation. Epilepsy is relatively rare in this subgroup.

Medication

Some prepubertal children with autism are given various kinds of medication, including anti-epileptic drugs. These usually have some effect, not only on undesirable symptoms but also on behaviour and academic functioning in school.

Neuroleptics

Most prepubertal children are not treated with drugs such as haloperidol (Haldol) or pimozide (Orap) because of the relatively high risk of unwanted effects of these drugs on the nervous system. However, occasionally they are needed even in this young age group, usually to decrease hyperactivity or self-destructive behaviour. They reduce such behaviours and often have some positive effects on socialization and learning, but the benefits in these latter areas often do not outweigh the hazards. From the age of adolescence, motor overactivity, self-injury, general 'nervousness' or apathy all seem to respond well or moderately well to such drugs and they are often used in the treatment of these particular symptoms. Some of these drugs have a blunting effect on cognition, but careful study has revealed this to be a rare phenomenon and it is seldom a cause of cessation of medication. Sedation may be more common (as may weight gain, particularly with thioridazine (Melleril) medication) and is sometimes perceived as a major obstacle to academic progress.

New or 'atypical' neuroleptics, such as risperidone and clozapine, may be useful when medication for aggression and other severe behaviour problems is required. However, risperidone often induces weight gain and clozapine may cause severe blood disease (albeit very rarely), meaning that only highly specialized experts should prescribe and monitor medications of this kind.

Antidepressants

Antidepressants have been used occasionally in autism, often with limited success. However, the use of the new serotonin reuptake inhibitor drugs such as fluoxetine, fluvoxamine and aitalopram may change this perspective. It appears that, at least in high-functioning autism, such drugs may have positive effects on hypoactivity and obsessions and compulsions and other ritualistic behaviour.

Lithium

Lithium has been tried in some studies of children with autism and has produced some worthwhile results in individual cases. From adolescence, lithium is sometimes very helpful in controlling mood swings and episodes of severely disturbed behaviour. There is a need to monitor the blood levels of this drug at regular intervals in order to prevent the development of toxic levels. With careful follow-up, the risks involved in lithium treatment are small. Occasionally, hypofunction of the thyroid gland may develop, but this can be treated effectively. Increased urine volumes and slight tremor are among the most commonly noted side-effects.

Anti-convulsive drugs

Carbamazepine (Tegretol, Hermolepsin) and valproic acid (Ergenyl, Orfiril) are the two anti-epileptic drugs which, so far, have been used with the most success and with the lowest frequency of major side-effects. Sometimes they may have a positive effect not only through the reduction of seizures, but also by improving psychological functioning. Nevertheless, both drugs may have side-effects such as skin rashes, drowsiness, decreased academic performance and gastrointestinal problems. Occasionally, carbamazepine may cause an increase in ritualistic and compulsive behaviours.

Older drugs such as phenytoin and phenobarbital should be used with great caution if at all. They appear to have a much higher rate of severe side-effects than the newer drugs. Benzodiazepines (such as clonazepam and nitrazepam) are sometimes very effective in reducing seizure activity but may actually contribute to increased withdrawal and bizarre behaviours/ritualism in people with autism and autistic-like conditions. If possible, their use should be restricted, except in emergency situations (diazepam (Valium) may be very effective during an acute seizure, but should not be used for prophylaxis).

The newest drugs in the field, such as vigabatrine and lamotrigine have not been in use long enough for a general judgement to be made as to their appropriateness in the treatment of epilepsy in autism.

Central stimulants

Central stimulants can have beneficial effects on severe hyperactivity in autism, at least in individuals whose IQ is above 50. Side-effects are generally mild, but reduction of appetite can sometimes be severe.

Other drugs

Children with autism and autistic-like conditions often respond to medication in a paradoxical fashion. For instance, a drug given to induce sleep may instead lead to a hyperactive state. Recommended doses of many medications may have to be (greatly) exceeded. Parents and teachers may feel that the physician in charge is groping in the dark. Finding the right medication and correct dosage in autism is often extremely difficult and may involve months of trials of several different drugs. Everybody involved in helping/teaching the child needs to bear this in mind and have a lot of patience in the process of finding the best possible treatment.

Chapter 6
Education and Guidance of People with Autism: The Major Educational Starting Points

Herman is a 40-year-old man with mild mental retardation who suffers from autism. Although autism is a developmental disorder, for almost the whole of his life he has been treated as a 'mental patient'. He has endured several episodes in psychiatric institutions, and now lives in a small villa-system unit, together with mentally handicapped adults without autism.

In his unit he is the only autistic resident and he has a bad reputation on account of his behavioural problems, which include extreme passiveness during certain periods or extreme dependence on any of the teachers who happen to be in his vicinity. On other occasions he does nothing but scream, lash out and scratch and pull the wallpaper off the wall. If these behavioural problems last too long, he is 'allowed' back into the psychiatric unit for a while.

Although the communication of people with autism is 'different', the way in which the nonverbal Herman is approached is largely verbal. People often think that he has fully understood the instructions but is simply being stubborn or doesn't feel like doing it.

He once had a toy guitar on which he strummed for hours on end until it drove everyone mad. So they took it away from him, because otherwise he wouldn't do anything else.

Although social interactions for people with autism are extremely difficult, the emphasis in the unit is still on group experience and group activities. Herman usually prefers to be alone, but in the unit they hold the view that he must learn just like the others, cosily in a group, 'otherwise he will become even more autistic than he already is'.

Herman very often finds himself in situations which are too difficult for him to understand. A considerable amount of socialization is presumed and he is unable to fulfil these expectations. Owing to his difficulties with communication, he is unable to say he cannot cope.

His way of saying how difficult it all is, is by screaming, biting, and tearing the wallpaper off the wall. His behaviour says; 'I can't stand it any longer, it is too difficult'.

There are many people like Herman. Teachers who are not trained in autism are only human, after all. They may persevere for several (for both parties, difficult) years and then give up: they can no longer stay the course.

When we see how Herman spends a typical day in the unit, we start to understand some of the difficulties involved. The afternoon is the best period for him; then he has three hours in the workshop with an unbeliev-able luxury: an individual supervisor! Then Herman works, but because he has not learned to use any visual diagrams (even though he has capabil-ities for this because he recognizes photos without any problem) he is dependent for just about everything on the teacher. So he looks to him, and the teacher follows him, every afternoon, time and time again, a hundred times a day. Maybe Herman really thinks that this looking is expected of him, that it is an essential part of the work. But with so little independence he is in any event fairly helpless, even in that 'best period' of the day.

Fortunately for Herman, the unit has its own set of fixed routines, so he is able to predict the sequence of events — and that gives him something to hold on to. But there are weekends and holidays and, of course, unfore-seen changes which catch him unawares. He then resorts to hand-biting, as the scars on his left hand show. The teachers make yet another attempt to involve Herman in domestic activities: doing the washing, the dishes, clearing or laying the table. But it isn't easy. A concept like laying the table, no matter how simple it is for us, is something that Herman doesn't fully comprehend. He looks at the others and tries to do the same. But often he gets it wrong: too many plates, not enough glasses, forks on the right instead of the left...Really he should be able to 'see' what is expected of him, but the instructions are in words. 'Lay the table': now he knows how to begin but he cannot retain in his memory the rest of the words that he hears. He takes his courage in both hands and makes a confident start, but five seconds later the meaninglessness of the concept is staring right back at him again. That yawning chasm of aimlessness, lack of direction. He grinds to a halt, totally blocked. 'Look at him standing there again, the lazy-bones.'

But 'free' time is the most difficult of all for Herman, and unfortunately there are more than eight hours of free time each day. Sometimes he is urged to sit at the same table as the others and play cards, but he sits rocking back and forth. The nearness of all those other people, who are giggling and doing things which are mostly incomprehensible to him, is something he finds unbearable. Fortunately, the group leaders soon appreciated what is happening and Herman is no longer expected to join in the card games. The other residents of the unit also prefer that Herman no longer joins them.

Nevertheless, this doesn't solve the leisure problems. For Herman wants to do all sorts of things during his free time, but he doesn't know what, or how, or where, or for how long. And he is being consumed by the contradictory feelings of wanting to and not being able to. He sometimes screams, or tags along after the teachers, who also do not quite know how to interpret his extreme dependence, telling him to go back and sit down like everyone else. Frequently, it gets so bad that he simply has to explode: screaming, biting, and tearing the wallpaper off the wall...(Peeters 1994).

Herman is bored to tears. He needs attention but doesn't know how to demand it. He wants to be occupied, but he doesn't know how. He has 'behavioural problems'. Each time he starts to bang his head against the wall, someone on the staff comes running over to him. Something is happening! If he hits a fellow-resident on the head, the result is the same: there is the staff member again. After a few experiences he sees how to demand attention. In the unit the conclusion is reached that he displays self-destructive behaviour, that he is aggressive. It is decided that he needs help and the doctor is summoned.

In numerous institutions there are people like Herman. They may be cared for with great dedication and energy, but without specialization in autism and frequently understaffed. The story often does not have a happy ending. For years, attempts are made to help until the time comes when it is no longer possible and medication then has to be used compensate for the lack of care specialized in autism.

A behavioural problem is merely the tip of the iceberg which has a huge invisible mass under the water. Herman's behavioural problems are also something like the tip of the iceberg in that the causes lie much deeper; and it is the cause that has to be treated. Symptomatic treatments bypass the causes and have merely short-term effects: they are emergency procedures.

Nevertheless, it is emergency procedures which are mostly used in units for adults with autism; after all, the staff involved in helping/teaching have usually had no specific training in autism. Summoning the doctor and administering medication seems to be the only possibility when staff feel they have to do something.

And yet what Herman really needs is an alternative form of communication: if he cannot speak, then he can surely learn to use a card with the message 'help' or (I want) 'bingo' or 'work' or 'room'. He needs a communication programme. Herman also wants more pursuits and activities during the day. Teachers must develop more specially adapted work activities for him, encourage appropriate work behaviour and a repertoire of leisure skills. In other words, Herman needs an educational programme tailored to someone with autism. The best strategy for the treatment of behavioural problems is prevention, and education specialized in autism is prevention.

What has happened is that an attempt has been made to fit Herman, although with the best of intentions, into the patient care system, instead of the other way round. The relationship between people with autism and most of today's professionals (with their defective or nonexistent preparatory education in autism) is something which can be compared with events in the Greek myth of Procrustes. Procrustes was a robber who forced travellers to lie on a bed and made them fit it, not by adapting the bed to them but the other way round. Someone whose legs were too long had bits cut off until he fitted properly in the bed. Someone whose legs were too short was stretched.

In the world of autism, too, we frequently still come across a similar concept. In the relationship of the 'strong' professional and the 'weak' person with autism the weak party is encouraged to adapt himself to the strong one.

Jan and the limited power of abstraction

At the age of seven Jan was still unable to talk and his parents requested explicit help to teach him to talk. His developmental profile is shown in Figure 3.

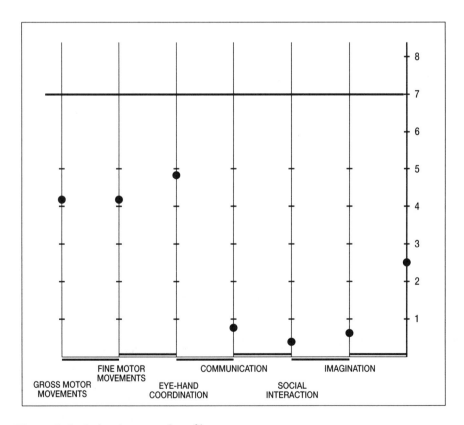

Figure 3. Jan's developmental profile

It can be seen from the figure that Jan has a chronological age of 7 years (the horizontal line), that he has a general developmental age of two and a half years (dot at extreme right), and that his motor skills (gross and fine motor movements, eye–hand co-ordination) are situated between 4 and 5 years. These are his 'islands of intelligence'; they are situated higher than his general developmental age, but they are nevertheless retarded (i.e. they are lower than his chronological age). Jan's development of the triad (communication, social interaction and imagination) is below a developmental age of 12 months, and it is precisely in these areas that the greatest demands are made on the power of abstraction.

Communication

Suppose that the teacher was not well informed about the specific difficulties in the development of the power of abstraction in people with autism. He might think that at two and a half years normal children talk, so if Jan is not yet talking, he must nonetheless be close. So the teacher focuses attention on a remedial programme of verbal imitation. Such an attitude would be 'cruel' to Jan. He would be asked too much and encouraged to achieve things far beyond his capabilities. Alternatively, the teacher may adopt a more cautious approach, and may think, 'In normal development a child first learns to recognize a picture before he speaks. So let us develop a system of communication using pictures'. Even that would have been beyond Jan's capabilities in that stage of his development. To teach Jan to communicate, it will be necessary to start at an even lower level; to be specific: at the object level (see below).

Social interaction

At two and a half years there is already a lot of reciprocal behaviour, not only with the parents but with peers. But Jan still doesn't understand that parents are good 'models'. Understanding people requires even more power of abstraction than is needed for communication, because human feelings such as tenderness, sorrow, anger and fear cannot be observed directly. They have to be deduced and analysed as to meaning.

How can you possibly know, as a hyperrealist, that the facial expression on the left in Figure 4 most probably means 'happy', and that the expression on the right most probably means 'sad'? And furthermore, do all people really express happiness and sorrow in precisely the same way, with exactly the same upward or downward curving of the corners of the mouth? This is typically something for surrealists once again.

Jan's parents are extremely worried about the difficult relationship they have with Jan. You can explain that since people with autism have a very literal perceptive mental set, they must also be 'socially blind'.

Figure 4. The facial expressions for happy and sad.

Imagination and play

Jan, according to his parents, doesn't play well with other children and he has difficulty keeping himself occupied in his free time. If you understand the triad of autism, then you will realize that matters can hardly be otherwise. As a case in point, let us see how much power of abstraction is needed to play 'normally', i.e. to spend one's free time meaningfully. To start with, in order to play with other children you must already understand the language, and for Jan this is impossible. Playing with other children requires that you understand the rules of the game. But even in the simplest of games, not all the rules are immediately perceptible. They have to be deduced. That calls for assistance from the analytical power of abstraction.

Even when Jan plays on his own, it is not easy for him. A jigsaw puzzle is okay — with that you don't have to deduce too much. You can see directly how the shapes fit together — the jigsaw pieces speak for themselves. But many other games that his parents buy in an ordinary toy shop are open-ended. What is expected of you is not immediately perceptible. You have to be able to see beyond things — that surrealism again, all that metaphysics!

The story of Jan shows how compensation strategies must be sought within the patient care system, making allowance for the inadequate power of abstraction of people with autism.

More on the level of abstraction

Take, for example, a car. I have a photo of a car, I have the written word 'car', I have a drawing of a car, and I have the spoken word 'car' (see Figure 5).

Any object can be represented by all kinds of symbols, including the actual object, pictures, and written and spoken words These representations will be addressed separately and considered in terms of the level of difficulty for people with autism.

Figure 5. Different representations of a car.

The spoken word

'Car', 'wagen', 'maquina', 'coche', 'voiture', 'automobile'; it can be seen that words are extremely abstract and not 'iconic': there is no immediately perceptible link between the sounds and their meaning, because in other languages we find different sounds for the same object. It can also be seen that verbal information is transient — I have hardly voiced the words and they have already gone. ('Verba volant, scripta manent' — spoken words fly, they cannot be held on to, Figure 6.)

People with autism are good at processing visuospatial information, but they are far less adept when it comes to transient, temporal information. Spoken words have no visuospatial features, and, furthermore, they are abstract. Processing spoken language calls for two complex information processing skills: transient and abstract.

The written/printed word

When you *see* the words 'car', 'wagen', 'maquina', 'coche', 'voiture' and 'automobile' and look at their features, you are brought to two conclusions:

Figure 6. Spoken words fly, they Cannot be held on to.

- written words are extremely abstract
- but they are less transient than spoken words.

They remain, they have a visuospatial character and a person with autism can take time to process them.

'When I heard the spoken language', says Temple Grandin (Grandin and Scariano, 1986) 'the words had no more meaning for me than other sounds. I only started to understand a few isolated words when I saw them in writing'.

'I began to understand what words are used for when I saw them printed on paper.' (Joliffe, Lansdown and Robinson, 1992).

In the literature on autism it is documented that people with autism are 'visual learners'. So it should come as no surprise to learn that there is a small group of people with autism who cannot speak but are able to express themselves better in writing or through the printed word. It is therefore understandable that some people with autism become discouraged when the style of education is verbal and teachers appeal to precisely those aspects which are the most difficult for them: auditory verbal information, which is too abstract and too transient.

Pictures/drawings/photos

During normal development, a time comes when the connection is made between an object and a picture. When I produce a photograph of a car you immediately see that there is an perceptible connection between the symbol and what is symbolized. Here is something that is somewhat more directly observable than a written word.

Is it a car? One look at the picture and most people will say, 'Yes, it is a car'. But *is* it a car? No. A great deal of conjuring is needed in order to comprehend a three-dimensional object (a real car) in two dimensions (a photograph) and then say, 'This is a car'. In that sense Magritte was right when he gave his famous painting of a smoker's pipe the title 'Ceci n'est pas une pipe' ('This is not a pipe'). Viewed from a hyperrealistic viewpoint he was right and we were surrealists by calling a picture of a pipe a pipe. Understanding a connection between the two makes an appeal to the same decoupling mechanism of which we spoke earlier. We must 'distance ourselves' from the concrete reality, make an appeal to our power of abstraction, and 'transcend' the literal. A photograph really only has a 'shallow' meaning. For a 'hyperrealist' this piece of 'surrealism' can demand too much cognitive effort. Nevertheless, information derived from drawings or photos is already less abstract than the written word; the information is also more visuospatial: the information can be 'held on to' longer, so that a person with autism can 'inflate' the shallow two-dimensional information cognizably into three dimensions.

Objects

An even more concrete manner of understanding and passing on information is through objects. If someone holds up the keys of a car and says, 'We are leaving', then he is communicating on an object level. In normal development, children of just one year of age already understand quite a few relationships between objects and subsequent events.

Figure 7. Is this a car? Yes, we say spontaneously. But *is* it really a car? No, but still… The real one is parked outside, and that is the one I will be driving off in later.

It is important that we realize that seeing a connection between a toy car (Figure 7) and a *real* car does require a cognitive effort of 'decoupling'. Just as a doll is a symbol for a human being, a toy car is a symbol for a real car, and, one must be able to see and understand the relationship. If you intend to use a toy car as a symbol for 'Lessons are over, you may now go home with the car', then you should make the association between the toy car and the event which is to follow. For a hyperrealist with autism and an extremely low intellectual age, that effort may be asking too much. A toy car is a toy car and that's the end of it. No conjuring tricks. That a toy car can 'say' 'We are leaving', and that an 'object vocabulary' exists (just as a vocabulary of words), are things that will have to be learned.

You should now have a better understanding of what type of 'conjuring trick' normal development is: without needing real lessons, a normal child spontaneously learns to understand the meaning of objects, of drawings and photographs, and of words, in an ever-rising curve of abstraction. This requires a tremendous amount of 'imagination'. Imagination in the primitive sense of the word: the talent to go beyond the physically perceptible, to understand the metaphysical connection between 'things' and their 'meaning'.

Maria and the language trap

Maria runs on like a mill race. When she sees bananas on the table in her hostel, she says, 'Mummy buys lots of bananas. Mummy buys two kilos of bananas. We have a lot of bananas at home. Bananas are yellow. Bananas come from Ecuador. Bananas come from Africa. Bananas come from Cuba'. What she would really like to say is, 'May I have a banana?', but the words simply do not come out.

The phenomenon of 'delayed echolalia' has already been addressed at some length. People with autism tend to relate words and phrases to certain situations without really understanding what they are saying. In the process of growing up, their technical speaking ability becomes greater. So people with autism often say more than they really understand. It is a phenomenon which often causes confusion in the patient care system, because it is assumed that people with autism always actually understand the questions they ask. However, the more you answer a number of 'why' questions from people with autism, for example, the more you confront them with their impotence and shortcomings. Attempts to explain things then have a contrary effect and make the chaos even worse. In people with autism you therefore frequently see two kinds of speech. On one hand, they may speak in very long sentences, with combinations of words which they 'borrow', but whose real content they do not understand so well. On the other hand they may speak in their own, self-created language which reflects their real understanding but, strangely enough, contradictorily gives an 'impoverished' impression.

The conclusion is obvious: despite the 'impressive' sentences that people with autism frequently utter, they need more help in understanding than we often suspect. This help comes largely through visual support.

Visual support helps in two ways. On one hand it supports communication from the environment *to* people with autism. The use of written words or pictures, for example, helps them to situate themselves within the abstract time, 'When do we do activities? How long do they last?' On the other hand, it supports communication *by* the person suffering from autism. Maria, for example, was given pictures to put in front of her on the table. Taking a card and giving it to the teacher makes it much easier for her to ask, 'May I have a banana?'

In some respects verbs are often a more complicated concept than nouns. In spoken or written form, a verb such as 'toothbrushing' is not only abstract but also implies a whole sequence of activities that are not readily apparent, but which are deduced from understanding the ultimate goal.

Compare this with our own experience with the verb 'drive' when we were learning to drive a car. Just imagine that the driving instructor had simply said, 'Drive'. We would have found that really too preposterous. We expected a 'job analysis' from him, that he would analyse the concept of 'driving' in sub-steps which we then had to follow (first insert the key in the ignition, then place your left foot on..., etc). It is helpful to think about this in order to understand that pupils with autism need job analyses for verbs which we find as simple as ABC. And that they need to 'see' the sub-steps which have to be followed, because understanding the ultimate goal is so much more difficult for them.

By way of illustration, here is a short dialogue between Thomas, a higher-functioning boy with autism, and his mother. It was caused by Thomas — again — having done something wrong:

Mother: 'But Thomas, I explained it to you!'
Thomas 'But Mother, how can I understand it if I don't see it?'

In a word, seeing is knowing.

Take the simple word 'toothbrushing' ('se brosser les dents', 'tandenpoetsen', 'lavarsi i denti'). One does not 'see' the resemblance between sounds and concepts. For many people, the abstraction level will have to be lowered and put into a sequence of operations:

1. I take a toothbrush, toothpaste and a glass.
2. I make the toothbrush wet.
3. I put toothpaste on it.
4. I rub from left to right over my teeth.
5. I rub from top to bottom over my teeth.
6. I rinse my mouth.
7. I put away my toothbrush.

No matter how simple these intermediate steps may seem, for many people with autism even this task analysis is too incomplete and imprecise. For example, it doesn't say what the pupil must do with the water once he has cleaned his teeth. How much toothpaste should he use? For how long should he clean them? For how long should he rinse his mouth?

And so on. The sequence of operations seems self-evident to us (we know the ultimate objective), but some people with autism do not understand the ultimate objective, or are unable to remember the sequence.

Take the adult with autism who had learned through task analysis to do the laundry and to put away the washing afterwards. His parents found all the washing, neatly folded, but still wet, in the airing cupboard. They had forgotten to tell him one essential intermediate step: when you have taken the laundry out of the washing-machine, you must first let it dry before you fold it.

Where alternative forms of communication are concerned, people often still think that it hinders speech development and that it is therefore better not to begin too soon with visual support. This misunderstanding would be less persistent if we had a better appreciation of the facts. First, the problem in autism is not only in 'speech' but all forms of communication; and second, a good many words spoken by people with autism are less well understood than we think.

Chapter 7
Training Professionals and Parents in Autism

Autism is special in a special way

People with autism have qualitative impairments, according to the definitions.

In *Mindblindness* (Baron-Cohen, 1995) the author suggests that understanding the social blindness of people with autism asks too much of our imagination. Can we understand, he wonders, what it is to have a knowledge of objects through echo-location? 'Yes' we nod. Rationally, we may understand what it means: 'to know about objects through echo-location'. But do we also understand its meaning with our heart or guts? I do not think so. We simply miss the experience. In autism the problem is similar. Rationally, we may understand what it means to suffer from social blindness, but we do not really understand what it means with our heart or guts. We are born with too much social intuition, we simply miss the experience.

Helping people with autism requires an extraordinary, almost impossible, effort of imagination. And as long at the political decision-makers fail to understand this, parents and professionals risk having to continue without the necessary forms of information and training.

This introduction deals with the distinction between the rational understanding of definitions of autism and the daily experience of people with autism and their parents and carers. This chapter will also make clear, I hope, why theoretical information, although very important, should be linked to practical training. In these practical training sessions parents and professionals learn to translate theory into everyday life experience where they must come up with practical solutions. Of course, this also means that those responsible for training should know about autism not only from books, but also from their work with children, adolescents and adults, and their families. Book learning is important, but tells only half the story.

'Ordinary people cannot understand why a mother allows her child to bang his head against the wall, or that she doesn't punish her child when he turns her bag upside-down in the supermarket trolley', writes M. Akerley, herself the mother of an autistic boy who has since grown to manhood (Akerley, 1988). Ordinary carers cannot understand this either. Ordinary carers are given ordinary training where they learn to help ordinary special children. Ordinary special children, for instance, are children with mental retardation but not autism. They have delayed development, but they do not have a different development. To help them, we use ordinary special means. Because their problems have to do with slower development, we simplify our expectations and use an easier communication style. Simplification may be the most important educational strategy in the help we give to these ordinary special people. But in the case of autism this strategy does not work, because someone with autism does not only have a slower development, but also has a different development. He is special in a very special way. He does not only need simplification, but also extra clarification. He needs a supported, augmentative approach, an educational style with lots of visual support.

Love and intuition are of course very necessary, but not sufficient if you want to help someone who is special in such a special way. Parents have experienced this in a dramatic way, especially during the early years, when they tried to understand the 'why' behind the sleeping problems, the lack of discipline, the lack of communication and social reciprocity. Why did the ordinary ways of helping and consoling not work? Why does their child not play as other children? And so on. The explanation turned out to be 'autism'.

Parents do not want the professionals who want to help their children to have to undergo the same helplessness and perplexity that they have experienced. Parents know now that there are practical answers to practical problems, although maybe not the definite answers that we would hope for (because in autism with each solution a new problem awaits). Parents want professionals trained in autism before they have responsibility for their children, instead of having to try by trial and error for years, as they themselves did. Parents wish professionals a better fate. Professionals do not need training only as in crisis-intervention (set up only when the situation has become unmanageable), but right from the beginning. Parents feel bad when they see that their children are being used as guinea-pigs. Without full training in autism, professionals risk being overwhelmed with the same bewilderment as parents.

The triad

Social interaction

'Why does he never look at me with love and affection? Why does he laugh when I am crying, instead of crying with me or asking why I am so sad? Why is he so nice with me when I wear a red ribbon in my hair, but not when I am wearing a blue one? When he cries and I want to comfort him and cuddle him in my lap, why does it make everything worse?'

Trained professionals know that this is typical behaviour for someone with autism. The person with autism has difficulties reading our eyes, gestures and attitudes. He has difficulty understanding what we feel, think and intend. He is too much of a 'behaviourist'. He has difficulties going 'beyond' the perception. Socially he seems blind. All this is 'normal' for someone with autism. (But the DSM-IV and ICD-10 definitions of autism merely mention 'Qualitative impairments in social interaction'.) Yet for a professional who is not trained in autism this behaviour is not 'normal'. Like parents, the professional may feel rejected, unrewarded for his efforts and it is possible that he may think, 'How self-centred, what a little monster, I'll let him see what he does to me...'. And before we know it someone is punished because he is handicapped.

Communication

When he is frustrated he says, 'The trains are leaving'. If he wants to sit on the swings, he says, 'There are no more oranges'. For days on end he sings 'choo-choo train', and if I take him to the station and show him a dozen trains and ask 'And what do you see now?' he says, 'Spaghetti with meat balls'.

This is all 'typical' behaviour for someone with autism, as the trained professional knows, but for someone who only knows about autism from books this may not be so obvious. (The DSM-IV definition talks about 'Qualitative impairments in verbal and non-verbal communication'.

Imagination. Repetitive stereotyped behaviour

'I put his bed in the other corner of the room. You should have seen him scream...' 'We decided not to eat pizza, like we usually do every Saturday...You should have seen him yell.' 'Or I say to him "Let us talk about last weekend's excursion", and instead he starts to talk about airplanes all over again, he knows all the companies and timetables, and if I ask him "Do you know why people travel to Barcelona?", he says', "To look at airplanes".'

DSM IV talks about a limited pattern of interests and stereotyped behaviour, and once again you think, 'What in the world is going on here?' You already know the answer: autism. Autism can be seen as a problem in the development of imagination. Imagination in the most rudimentary sense of the word: the talent to go beyond literal information, to add meaning to sounds and develop language; to add meaning to what you see and to develop social behaviour. And it is precisely in the areas of communication and social interaction where adding meaning is so important that people with autism fall back on a limited repertoire of stereotypical repetitive behaviour (Hermelin, 1976; Happé, 1994; Frith, 1989).

A pervasive developmental disorder

People with autism need lifelong protection, at different levels of help.

In the previous section the emphasis was put on understanding both in theory and practice the qualitative differences in communication, social interaction and imagination. The need for training is enormous since people with autism will have to live with these qualitative impairments all their lives. They will make progress but for most of them certain levels of help will continue to be necessary in their adult lives. Whether this help is offered in an environment with only other people with autism, or in a mixed environment, will be decided after analysis of the level of protection they need. But whether in a segregated or integrated environment the key question is whether they are surrounded by enough professionals who have been fully trained in autism.

The continuity of services that people with autism and their families need may be summarized as follows:

1. Diagnostic services.
2. Home-training services.
3. Preschool, primary school, adolescent classrooms, (day schools and/or boarding schools).
4. Work and living facilities for adults with autism.
5. Possibilities for leisure for people with autism and their families (especially during holidays and crisis periods).

In all these services professionals who are well-trained in autism are needed. In our society people seem to invest more readily in buildings than in training. We should focus on the fact that the quality of life of someone with autism depends more upon the way others can adapt to his difficulties than upon his own efforts. Remember that others have to try to share his mind, to try to understand what is difficult for him. Even though it is very challenging to try to imagine the world the way he sees it, it is easier than having him share others' minds.

The content of training

The five axes of professional training and education

'I moved his desk, you should have heard him ranting and raging.' 'Today we didn't eat chips as we usually do on a Monday, you should have heard him...' 'I thought, "Always the same, always those repetitions, surely that isn't normal for a child. I know what I'll do, I'll change his exercises. It'll be nice to do something creative." You should have heard him...' 'In our community, Christmas parties and carnival are very popular..., you should have heard him...' We give him environmental training. We don't want him merely to have armchair knowledge that he has learned from the textbooks. So after having explained to the class what a bank is and what you can do there, and what a post office is and what you can do there, we took him to a real post office and a real bank. Everything was shown to him. He seemed to be perfectly happy and imitated all he saw — a perfect lesson. On returning to school we decided to check it out once again. "So what is the difference between a post office and a bank?" "The post office has a sponge!" he replied. (He likes sponges, he licks sponges, he collects photos of sponges...)'

Ordinary teachers attend ordinary training courses where they learn how to help ordinary 'special' children. Ordinary special children are, for example, mentally handicapped children without autism. They have a delayed development, but in essence they are no different from us. To help these children teachers use special aids: as the essential problem is one of slower development, the teachers simplify their expectations, they use a simplified style of communication. Simplification is the most important pedagogical strategy in providing help for these ordinary special youngsters, but in the case of autism this strategy doesn't work, because an individual with autism not only has delayed development but also a 'different' development. He is specially special. He not only needs simplification, but also extra clarification. He needs an 'augmentative' approach, one with a great many visual aids. Love and intuition are essential, but they are not enough to help someone who is so specially special (Dewey, 1983). Parents discover this in a dramatic way, especially in the initial years, during the search for an appropriate diagnosis, for an explanation, for an understanding of the cause, and for a reason for so much apparently aggressive behaviour, lack of discipline, eating problems, sleeping problems, difficulties in communicating and lack of responding to normal forms of comforting.

Parents do not want teachers who wish to help their children to go through the same valley of tears they did. Parents now know that there are answers, although perhaps not definitive answers (because in autism, after each solution to a problem there is invariably a new one waiting to be solved). Parents want professionals to know what autism is before they see their child, to avoid them having to experiment and search for years — as most parents themselves have had to do, to their own detriment. Parents wish professionals a better fate. Professionals need to attend refresher courses (and not only when problems are already completely out of hand). For all students who might ever be required to give guidance to young people with autism, a minimum course of study on autism should be included in the core curriculum. And, furthermore, anyone wishing to help people with autism professionally (as an instructor, teacher, diagnostician, etc.) should be able to follow advanced training and education in order to specialize in autism, not just do a hasty patch and repair job.

The training and education embraces five axes. As you will see, they are so logical and self-evident that many professionals will ask themselves what is so new about them. The fact that these dimensions are so recognizable is really quite logical: autism is a developmental disorder, and within the scope of our training and education there are many parallels with the guidance of other children with a developmental disorder. Besides these similarities, however, there are nevertheless quite a few differences which are too easily overlooked. It so happens that autism is a 'pervasive' developmental disorder; children with autism are not only mentally retarded, they are, above all, different. So professionals must understand that difference.

The first axis

The first training and education axis consists of a sound theoretical knowledge of autism. (This is only logical: someone who is made responsible for the training and education of a blind person must understand the effects of blindness on development, otherwise he himself will be responsible for quite a few emotional and behavioural problems.) This theoretical grounding embraces aspects of diagnosis and definition. It demonstrates why the 'different' communication (see definition) of people with autism necessarily requires a 'different' training and education (each type of training and education, whether in self-help, work skills or leisure skills, has as its starting point the notification of expectations, the hope of being understood, i.e. communication).

The different 'social' characteristics mean that group training and education for pupils with autism may possibly be too difficult as a starting point (this is an important message for special education, where there is (justifiably) a long tradition of faith in group activities). People with autism who finish up in group situations where too high requirements are set run the risk of responding with behavioural problems. With a concept such as 'integration', therefore, one should exercise caution. It is not a means in itself. It is the ultimate goal of successful training and education. It is better to place the young person with autism in a school situation which is maximally adjusted to his handicap. Initially he is in greater need of protection than integration (Mesibov, 1988, McHale and Gamble, 1986; Volkmar, 1986).

Anyone who works with autistic youngsters and doesn't understand autism will, notwithstanding all his efforts and good intentions, through his lack of adaptation, place the child in situations that are too difficult for him and this will cause behavioural problems. That is simply the way it is: a child with autism not only needs love but also 'professional skill'. Parents know this better than anyone. They know how their normal expressions of tenderness are frequently rejected by a 'special' child.

Certain behavioural characteristics (stereotyped, repetitive behaviours, a proclivity for immutability...) teach us that people with autism have highly pronounced difficulties with the transfer of skills from one situation to another, from one person to another. As we ultimately do not learn in order to get good grades, but rather to facilitate and enrich our lives, teaching staff have to make a special effort to co-operate with parents, among other things in connection with the generalization of skills. This co-operation is not a luxury, not merely being polite — it is a professional necessity.

The second axis

The second axis consists of training in patient assessment as a basis for an individualized programme of education. This is necessary in view of the reputation of 'untestability' of pupils with autism, but this axis in itself is not so innovative. A person who works with a 'blind' pupil realizes that a general knowledge of blindness is not enough; one must also get to know the pupil as an individual, with all his unique characteristics. By the same token, this also applies to education for all handicapped pupils, but in the case of autism there are additional reasons which make a good assessment so imperative (Mesibov, Troxler and Boswell, 1988; Schopler and Mesibov, 1988). One of these is the very disharmonious development of pupils with autism.

In an 'ordinary mentally retarded pupil' of 9 years of age, for example, with an intellectual age of 4 years, the teacher can presume that he functions for all 'subjects' as a 4-year-old. He has the body of a child of 9, but he feels, lives and thinks as a child of 4. In an 'autistic mentally retarded pupil' this is not so. In his case, examination will demonstrate that he has a far more unstable learning profile. A 9-year-old with an intellectual age of 4, for example, but with an 'island of intelligence' in eye–hand co-ordination (where he performs as a 5-year-old), but with less language, and symbolic play and the social understanding of a child of 2. The teacher will therefore have to have a much more detailed insight into each separate area of development. Otherwise there is every likelihood that he will underestimate or overestimate the child, thereby making the situation intolerably difficult for him. Then he is 'not amenable to education'.

A second argument to demonstrate the necessity of a good examination is the deficit of generalization skills of the autistic child. With his inadequate conceptual development he does not spontaneously recognize that a skill learned in one context can also be applied in other contexts. His level of skills can therefore be different in one context than in others. Here, too, it is important to gain an insight into this through examination. So you see: the importance given to examination is not new, but in autism this examination must be particularly thorough. A person who lacks good examination data as the starting point of a treatment runs the risk of having expectations which are either too high or too low and, because of that, may unintentionally cause behavioural problems.

The third axis

The third axis consists of adaptation of the environment to the handicap. Again, this axis is in itself not innovative, it is entirely recognizable. The development of the Braille system is an adaptation of the environment which enhances the quality of life of a blind person. Is there a system for autism? Can the quality of life of a person with autism be enhanced by adapting the environment? Fortunately, the answer is yes. Normal as well as mentally retarded children (but then on a delayed level) have sufficient creativity 'to go beyond the information given', as Bruner calls this innate biological talent (Bruner, 1973). Thanks to this ability, they develop in a fairly playful way communication, social understanding and play behaviour. Pupils with autism suffer from an extremely literal mental set; they have far more difficulty with the addition of meaning to their observations than their intellectual age leads one to suspect. They are 'behaviourists' (Frith, 1989). We can help these behaviourists by communicating our expectations in a less abstract manner. The autistic pupil will then not only become more independent, but also find more emotional security and meaningfulness in life. Just as we talk of 'alternative communication' for someone who cannot speak, we can talk of the development of 'alternative signification' for someone who can find no significance in normal communication. Through the organization of the class and by making abstract periods of time predictable (children with autism also have need of time management; they are lost in time, so we develop for them alternative class workbooks and clocks, as appropriate). Conceptual significance being replaced by perceptual significance is one way of looking at it. A meaning in life is something none of us can do without, but for youngsters with autism very drastic adaptations are needed to add meaning to their lives. Again, this axis of adaptation is recognizable and logical, but the adaptation of the environment to the handicap of autism has to be different, because autism is different.

The fourth axis

The fourth axis has to do with functionality. We not only have to start somewhere with the process of training and education by making use of good examination data, we also have to know the direction we want to go.

Children soon become adults. We must prepare them for the happiest, most independent adulthood possible by putting the emphasis on skills which they will then need most. These include communication, work skills and work behaviour, self-help and domestic skills, leisure and social skills and (functional) academic skills (Fredericks *et al.*, 1983; Mesibov, 1988; Peeters, 1987).

We shall have to be selective in this regard, because people with autism will have only those functional skills which they have been explicitly taught. Consideration should primarily be given to the application of skills in everyday life and not learning things automatically by heart. The rain man in the film of the same name was brilliant with figures and calculations (doing mental arithmetic) but he could not use his knowledge of figures to handle money or do the shopping. People with autism, even the better-functioning ones, are frequently impractical: they have great difficulty in applying the knowledge they have in their head in the social domain.

The fifth axis

The fifth axis is concerned with 'how': the manner of training and education should be adapted to autism. Again, the axis is logical: special education has been developed for blind and for deaf people. Developing and applying an analogue system for pupils with autism is perhaps the greatest challenge, because no one is prepared for it in 'traditional' special education. Nevertheless, auto-educational strategies have their own specificity. Each individual pupil must be helped in a different way.

Special education which offers the type of teaching used in mental retardation (which consists principally of simplification) does not suffice, because a person with autism is not only mentally retarded but — as already mentioned — he finds it extremely difficult to transcend the literal (these difficulties are situated at various levels of intelligence). As a result, they need additional clarification by way of compensation (teachers help them to understand meanings which remain inaccessible to them in the normal way). Pupils with autism are 'visual thinkers' and, even those with high IQs need visual support (Grandin, 1992; Joliffe, Lansdown, and Robinson, 1992).

These axes have to be learned through training which combines theory with practice.

Types of training

Awareness training and 'pre-training'

A broad group of professionals need to have up-to-date general knowledge about autism. All students choosing a career where they may have contact with people with autism or related disorders should have a general knowledge that would at least allow them to suspect or screen for the possibility of autism and to refer the person for more specialized diagnosis and educational help. In many countries parents and their children lose years because professionals have the clichéd image of the self-absorbed child and do not understand that the 'active but odd' subgroup has the triad of difficulties that make up autism.

We should not forget that persons within the autism spectrum are not a minority group, as many claim. A recent epidemiological survey shows an incidence of 1 in 1000. If one starts with an educational definition of autism the incidence is 2 in 1000. If one includes all the spectrum disorders or autistic-like conditions the incidence is 0.6–1% of the general population of school-age children (Steffenburg, 1990). In summary, it seems that autism and its spectrum disorders are more common than previously estimated. It means, among other things, that practically every general practitioner will have people with autism or with disorders of its spectrum among his patients. Also, professionals such as speech therapists, occupational therapists, teachers and psychologists are extremely likely to come into contact with people with autism. In most European countries autism continues to be underdiagnosed and, as a consequence, people with autism and their families do not get the help they need and therefore suffer more than necessary.

Another argument, besides the need to encourage a greater theoretical understanding of autism and its educational treatment, is that autism contains so many messages for the treatment of people suffering from other disorders. At a general level we have seen how, in the history of autism, professionals who specialised in 'minor' problems of, for example, communication, were not prepared to deal with 'major' communication problems.

But it does work the other way: professionals who specialise in autism do have a certain facility for developing forms of treatment of 'minor problems' of imagination, social understanding and communication. In Belgium I heard an inspector of special education say that the autism project is the best thing that has ever happened to special education since its foundation. Many schools with classrooms for children with autism are now also applying visual support and other educational strategies with their mentally retarded or hyperkinetic children. We consider a 40-hour course is worth the investment.

A specialized training programme

The Center for Training on Autism was founded 18 years ago, because specialized training programmes for parents and professionals were not available. Since then thousand of professionals have been trained in Belgium and in most European countries. This training has included theoretical introductions, practical training, specialized training in assessment, the adaptation of the environment and communication. So although much important and necessary work has been done it is still not enough. What has been done was more or less crisis intervention and this is what has to change.

In more and more European countries autism is now recognized as a handicap, and that at least is progress. But in no European country that I know of are professionals trained in autism when they start working with the autistic population. In this way parents and children remain vulnerable. Too much still depends upon the goodwill of professionals, directors and decision-makers. We must work towards a future where professionals who chose to work with autism can be given full training immediately and obtain a diploma in autism after completing their studies. We have to get away from a system where people think of training as something to be used in periods of deep crisis only. Such training is necessary too for professionals who, with no previous preparation, are being asked to 'treat' people with autism.

For example, recently a professional told me that he was asked to take responsibility for the therapy of an adolescent girl with autism, for half an hour each afternoon. He accepted after protesting mildly, 'What is autism? What shall I do?' He was told that people with autism do not want to speak, so you must make them speak, and the best way to do that was to start talking and not to stop until the half hour was over. The professional said, 'After one minute the girl started shaking all over her body and sighing "aah,aah,aah,aah...". Her behaviour became worse and worse, but I felt I had to keep talking to her until the 30 minutes were up'. This is not a joke. The list of mental atrocities in autism is endless. An ethical code describing necessary forms and ways of treatment must be developed. Parents all too often have the impression that their children are being experimented upon and used as guinea-pigs. What would you say if you had lung problems but were being treated by a dentist ('Oh, but we shall be sending him to a lung congress'). We think that training should consist of at least 300 hours and be a combination of theoretical and practical work.

Post-training and follow-up

Due to the difficulty professionals have in going beyond literal information, and their somewhat rigid cognitive style, they very often show echo-behaviours. Instead of using a personal creative language they echo words and phrases. This is called echolalia. Some children are so motivated to be like us that they kiss everyone they meet. We call this behaviour echopraxia. Literal imitation of social behaviour is typical for 'active but odd' people with autism. Thomas, a high-functioning child with autism, has seen a magician on television who put his scarf on the table and said that he would make a rabbit appear. 'Hocus, pocus. A rabbit'. Since then Thomas has tried it himself several times, 'Watch, I'm going to make a rabbit appear from under my scarf. Hocus, pocus. Then he takes away the scarf, and when he sees that there is still no rabbit, he says in a very disappointed way, 'I still cannot do it'. This is 'echo-play'.

Echo-behaviour is not only typical of autism, it is typical for anyone facing a challenge that is too big for them. Professionals who attend theoretical and practical training sessions and then go back to work often exhibit echo-behaviour. This is normal. The very individualized programme and adaptations they have seen during the practical training sessions can be taken and carried out too literally. To understand the 'qualitative differences' in autism in general is already challenging enough, but then to take into account all the individual differences among children makes it even more complex. Taking educational strategies as a recipe is a typical and 'normal' echo-behaviour in professionals. What they need is help from outside. Such help, offered by an autism team with years of experience, may help them to learn more about individualization and help to avoid burn-out, so typical of people who live under extremely demanding circumstances (just ask parents). Without regular consultation from such a specialized team the motivation and quality of education may diminish. Professionals also need an objective look from outside from time to time for supplementary assessment or to help them to rethink a certain situation.

Training in autism is never finished. If learning about autism does not expand, it contracts. Regular in-service training and other forms of post-training are not a luxury but a necessity.

Training parents

If one thinks of training one thinks first of the needs of the professional, but parents are of course most directly concerned with the individual with autism. We must be aware that understanding autism and adapting to their child does not come spontaneously to parents either. Parents need the best information about autism possible, they need home-training that focuses on autism (otherwise 'help' is more of a burden than a relief) and they need support if they want in-depth training in communication and other key subjects. Training where professionals and parents learn to collaborate is really the kind of training that is needed most. For such collaboration and for the generalization of skills it is necessary for parents and professionals to have similar views on autism. For the 'political' programme of autism, this is pushing the authorities to create the continuous lifelong services that specialize in autism, for which task parents need to be well informed about autism.

If one looks at the development of services in many countries it is clear that very often the best services are found in regions where parents have been most active. The future of people with autism may depend to a great extent on the levels of activity and awareness and training of parents. Parents' societies need to help professional organizations to push the authorities towards developing the pre-training, specialization and post-training that I have described. Without their help the authorities may suspect trainers to be advocates of their own careers when they plead for full training programmes for professionals.

Extraordinary youngsters require extraordinary professionals

The profile of a carer

Sixteen years of experience in training forces us to formulate another striking insight: in order to help these different youngsters with autism, professionals themselves must be a little bit 'qualitatively different' themselves. Some carers will never be able to develop individualized educational programmes, even though they have followed the best possible theoretical and practical training. It is useless to 'force' someone to work with autistic children (we know examples where directors randomly appoint teachers and it just does not work). Professionals must choose autism themselves. They do not choose 'in spite of autism', but 'because of autism'.

What is the secret? Until now we have always said, for want of another explanation, that one needs to be bitten by the bug of autism. For insiders this is perfectly clear. We know professionals who will never be bitten by the bug — who are immune to it. The problem is that bugs are invisible to the authorities. So we think that developing a professional profile for carers in autism is necessary.

The most important characteristics include the following.

1. To be attracted by differences. We think that it helps to be a 'mental adventurer' and to feel attracted to the unknown. Some people fear differences, other people are attracted and want to know more about them.
2. To have a vivid imagination. As said previously, it is almost impossible to understand what it is like to live in a literal world, to have difficulty in going 'beyond the information', to love without inborn social intuition. In order to be able to share the mind of someone with autism, who suffers from a lack of imagination, we must have enormous levels of imagination in compensation.
3. To be able to give without getting an (ordinary) thank you. We need to be able to give without receiving much back in return, and not to become disappointed by a lack of social reciprocity. (With experience we will learn to detect alternative forms of 'thank you'. Also, parents usually provide ample compensation.)
4. To be willing to adapt one's natural style of communication and social interaction. The style to use is more linked to the needs of someone with autism than to our spontaneous levels of social communication. This is not easy and requires many efforts of adaptation, but, after all, whose needs are we serving?
5. To have the courage 'to work alone in the desert'. Especially at the beginning of the development of appropriate services, few people understand autism, and a motivated professional risks being criticized instead of applauded for his enormous efforts. (Parents experienced this kind of criticism much earlier, ' all he needs is discipline', 'if he were mine', 'cool mothers', ...etc.).
6. Never to be satisfied with how much one knows. Learning about autism and educational strategies is a continuous process. 'The professional who thinks he has found it, has lost it.' Training in autism can never be completed.

7. To accept that each bit of progress brings a new problem. People have a tendency to abandon puzzles if they cannot solve them. This is impossible in autism. Once you start, the 'detective' work is never over.
8. Besides teaching skills, the professional needs extraordinary didactic capacities. He needs to take very small steps and to use visual support at a very individualized level. There are so many evaluations to be made, one has to adapt all the time.
9. Be prepared to work in a team. Because the approach needs to be coherent and co-ordinated, all professionals need to be informed about the efforts of others and the levels of help they provide.
10. Be humble. We may be experts in autism in general, but parents are the experts about their own children and we need to take into account their wisdom. The professional who wants to remain 'on his pedestal' is not needed in autism. When collaborating with parents it is important to talk about successes, but also to admit failures and to ask for help. Parents need to learn that an expert in autism is not an Olympic god.

Some will wait for the word 'love' in this list. Love is of course essential, but, as one parent warned, love is not a miracle cure. Parents and professionals who count too much on the effects of love, will be disappointed. If the child does not make enough progress, is it because he had not been loved enough? Or perhaps we have loved enough, but he has not accepted our love sufficiently. Such attitudes are destructive and create an abyss where what is necessary is optimal collaboration (Dewey, 1983). *Omnia non vincit Amor* (love *doesn't* conquer all). Autism is different.

If a 'strong' professional wishes to help a 'weaker' fellow citizen, then he should adapt himself, not the other way round. Being able to help therefore presupposes:

1. An understanding of autism.
2. Being able to start on the basis of examination.
3. Being able to adapt the environment.
4. Being able to emphasize extremely functional skills;
5. Using a style of communication during the training and education process which is specialized in autism.

Chapter 8
Education and Guidance of People with Autism: Practical Examples

To be as happy as possible (according to parents) a person with autism should have the following.

1. A certain amount of predictability in his life, not the feeling that life is controlled by fortuity.
2. Be able to express himself, have developed a specially adapted system of communication.
3. Be able to take care of himself as well as possible. To be able to get himself dressed and undressed, to wash himself, prepare meals and handle money. In other words, to develop self-help and domestic skills.
4. Be able to spend his waking hours usefully. Be able to work, because if he has nothing to do for too long he becomes extremely troublesome and unhappy. Work skills and work behaviour should therefore be developed.
5. Teach himself to occupy his free time. Not everything can be planned and foreseen. He himself must learn to develop initiatives during non-organized time. Leisure skills must be developed.
6. Learn to associate with others and enjoy their company. This is the domain of social skills.

The start of special education in autism, the start of specialized prevention of behavioural problems in autism, is based on the understanding that everyone needs predictability in his life.

A person with autism once wrote: 'Since life consists of such a confusing mass of sights and sounds, for a person with autism it is a real help if he can get some order into his life'. And further, 'For me it is of vital importance that there are well-defined places and times' (Joliffe, Lansdown, and Robinson, 1992).

It is important that we have information in connection with our 'where' and 'when' questions. Normally we don't really give it a moment's thought. In our daily life we have our routines and know where we eat, where we sleep...but in a strange environment (where people speak another language, for example) those are the first things we worry about. Where do I sleep? Where do I eat? Where is the cinema? Where do I have to work? When do I start work? When do we have a break? When do we eat? When is the working day over? And we want that information in a language we can understand. In brief, predictability means having an idea, or a mental image, of 'where' and 'when'. The answer to the question 'how long?' has been found to be of particular importance in this respect.

Communication, self-help and domestic skills, work skills and work behaviour, and leisure and social skills are the key areas that are worked on in an educational programme which aspires to give the greatest possible level of happiness permitted by the limitations of autism. To learn these skills people with autism will need, above all, visual support.

The importance of visual support is evident in the following areas.

1. It offers predictability in space and, above all, in time.
2. It aids the development of communication.
3. It aids the development of the 'key subjects' (self-help and domestic skills, work skills and work behaviour, leisure and social skills, and school-oriented functional skills).

Where?

Imagine for a moment that I have invited someone with autism to come and join me at my table. He doesn't know me. He is a bit nervous. (For what kind of things do strangers do? They ask you to do things which you hardly understand, if at all; they take you with them and you have absolutely no idea where you are going; they ask you questions.) No sooner has he seated himself at my table than I bring out my lemonade and biscuits (I have been told that he has a special liking for them). The ice is broken. The next day I invite him back: lemonade and biscuits. He clearly begins to loosen up a little towards me. But I am new to autism and I do not know that people with autism soon make fixed associations, find 'details' self-evident and that they are hyperselective in their attention. Again I invite him to take a seat at my table. I give him a few jobs which I would like him to do for me. I have the intention of being very friendly, of encouraging him during the work I have asked him to do. Yet after three minutes I see that he is having a tantrum. What I don't understand is that he feels that he has been 'cheated' by me. The table 'told' him 'biscuits and lemonade', and now the same table 'tells' him 'work'. There are no certainties in life. Again, he doesn't have life under control and in his eyes, I am a liar.

In an educational programme we try to let the subjects, the furniture, the areas 'speak for themselves', so that their 'meaning' does not have to be deduced. We wish to proffer certainties by creating a predictable link between places, activities and behaviours. There are obvious areas which are used only for work (where you therefore expect a work behaviour) and others which are used only for free time (and there you expect less active effort). Offering a person with autism this predictability, contributes to the prevention of behavioural problems.

When?

We all have calendars, diaries and watches to make that abstract concept of time visible. Without these 'concretizations', many of us would feel rather lost. Just like us, people with autism have a need to situate themselves in time, to 'see' the time. (Only many of these forms of time management are still beyond the mental reach of most people with autism, the time still has to be deduced on a level which is too abstract. As a result, most people with autism, without additional help from us, feel lost in that sea of time.) If they cannot 'see' the time, they will often try to develop routines and rituals by way of compensation. They want all activities to be undertaken in the same sequence every day. In other words they want to get their life more under control, to build up their own predictability. And if the sequence of activities changes on a certain day, then they have 'behavioural problems'. However, our experience shows us that people with autism can also cope with changes in timetables, provided that they are able to anticipate those changes.

Isn't that the same for us? If we are looking forward to an important event and someone changes the 'programme' without telling us, we also find it difficult to accept. But it is much less difficult if we are able to foresee the changes.

The level on which we offer someone the concretization of time is highly individualized, dependent upon his abstraction competence. It is also important to realize that there is an evolution in forms: someone who once started on an object level may later use a picture level, perhaps also written 'time messages'. The important thing is not to aim for the highest level of abstraction *per se*, but for the highest level of independence.

There are daily schedules, for instance, (let us limit ourselves to that here, although some people also need, just as we do, weekly schedules and yearly schedules) using objects, a combination of both objects and drawings, drawings, photos, drawings/photos with printed text, and printed text only. These 'schedules' can be pinned up in a permanent place in the classroom or in the community. A number of people with autism also learn to use portable systems: printed or photographic information in workbooks. Getting a bit of order and predictability into the life of a person with autism is what it comes down to: offering 'pegs' on which to hang uncertainty.

Even people with autism who can speak, often benefit more from visual than from verbal information about time. As mentioned previously, much of the language has an echo-character, and cannot be analysed sufficiently as to meaning. Even when people with autism can speak, they have more trouble than may be suspected in using that language for making plans, ordering their life, or supporting their everyday activities.

Another way of explaining that 'instability' of language is by referring to the difference between 'external' and 'internal' language. The Russian psychologist Vygotsky points out how children at play frequently talk out loud to 'steer' or control their play. That language is subsequently internalized. 'Internal language' can be regarded as a repertoire of concepts which help us to organize and steer our behaviour. We 'know' how certain operations are put together and this internal awareness helps us to perform those tasks.

However, there is reason to believe that people with autism have far fewer internal scenarios like this (as already mentioned, their speaking is far more echo-like than we think and their understanding is less developed than their speech leads one to suspect. 'Internal language' can therefore be of less help to them (Halliday, 1973).

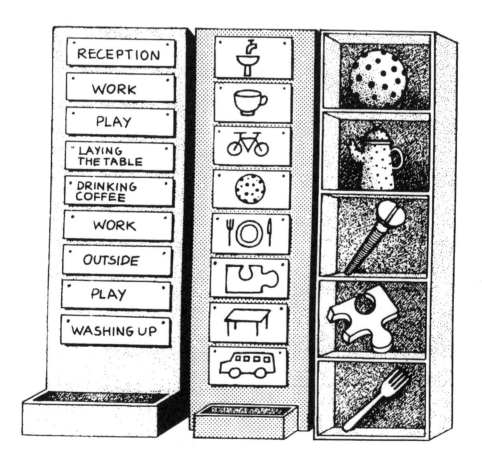

Figure 8. A visual daily schedule

The development of a visual daily schedule (and other forms of visual aid) which we discuss can therefore be regarded as an external scenario which serves to compensate for the inadequate internal scenario.

There are, for example, quite a few pupils who can speak who ask 100 times a day, 'When are we going to eat?', or 'When are we going home?'. And each time you reply, 'in an hour', 'later', or 'at four o'clock'. But less than a minute later it starts all over again, 'when are we going.?'

Sometimes they will have understood 'at four o'clock', but they have difficulty in retaining this transient information for any length of time in their memory, and certainly not in a manner stable enough to regulate their behaviour accordingly. It helps, however, if you can convey that information visually by asking them to look at their daily schedule. Here they can see the picture of 'work', then 'physical education', then there is a 'snack', after which they go home.

Scattered under the 'when' rubric you see visualized daily schedules of differing levels of abstraction, on subject level if necessary. On a higher abstract level, if they are up to it, a 'permanently anchored' schedule or a portable system, can be used.

Sometimes only a few activities can be announced instead of half a day or a full day. Offering too little predictability may cause behavioural problems, but offering more information than can be processed will only make them more confused and restless. It is a question of individualization.

Other individualizations are related to the use of symbols. Do they look at the symbols and do they put them away afterwards, or is it necessary that they keep the symbols with them as they go from one activity to the other? (The slightest distraction *en route* and some of them no longer remember what they are doing...) We shall not elaborate further on weekly schedules, monthly schedules or annual calendars. It goes without saying that these are also used as much as possible within the individual constraints of people with autism. Intermediate forms (both drawings and text, objects and pictures together) and time indicators of a more mobile nature (workbooks, 'auti-clocks') are likewise not discussed within the limited scope of this book.

How long?

How long? We look at our watch. If someone were to sit me at a table to do a job which I don't particularly like doing, then I would certainly like to know for how long I was expected to do it. When I have to 'wait' for quite a long time on another 'difficult' occasion ('indefinite waiting' is difficult not only for people with autism), for example, for a bus or a tram, then I consider it a great luxury if there is an electronic notice-board showing the number of minutes still left to wait. Information like that reduces nervousness and enhances the quality of life. This is certainly the case for someone who has greater difficulty than I do with processing time. Figure 9 shows a 'kitchen' programme with written information. How long do I have to work in the kitchen? Until the four activities are finished. Imagine that you were to give this information orally. Many people would have trouble retaining this much information for long enough in their memory. With the written words you have the instructions in a less transient form and you can fall back on them. It is an exterior scenario to compensate for the less well-developed interior scenario. The pictures and written words do not yet tell you how you must perform the activities (for that we shall develop other scenarios later on); they announce only the duration.

10.00	WASH UP / KITCHEN	
10.30	SWEEP THE FLOOR/LIVING-ROOM	
10.45	TAKE DUSTBIN OUTSIDE / GARAGE	
10.50	WATER THE PLANTS/DINING-ROOM	

Figure 9. A kitchen programme in written form (this information can of course be entered in a workbook).

Figure 10 shows the same scenario on a less abstract level, with drawings. For someone who has no conception of numbers and duration, it is important that he can 'see' the duration. Once again, visuospatial information replaces transient abstract concepts. Here the scenario is on the object level. Figure 10 is an example of a kitchen scenario. In the same way, you can develop leisure scenarios and any other type of activity scenarios.

For people with autism you normally start in a very simple way with 'work' schedules, the reason being that on a workbench you can offer the easiest activities. On a workbench you can also shield them in the best possible way from forms of stimulation which are not relevant to the job in hand.

The adult with autism for whom the work schedule in Figure 11 was drawn, liked colouring so much it was used as a reward and the symbol for colouring was incorporated into the schedule. This gave him a greater incentive to work. Furthermore, he saw that he could continue with his colouring later on. Each symbol in the figure stands for just one activity that has to be carried out. The pupil/person with autism picks the number (the colour, drawing) and takes it to the box on the rack with the same number.

A work schedule on an object level is shown in Figure 12. The person with autism learns that each box on the left symbolizes an activity which has to be carried out. The more boxes, the more work. When all the boxes have 'disappeared', i.e. have been moved to the right, the work is finished.

Naturally, the organization from left to right is something that he has to learn, but that is not too difficult to understand: left is 'to be done', right is 'done'. Is that left–right sequence really important? Just try to decipher the following:

LEFT-RIGHT ORGANIZATION

THGIR OT TFEL MORF GNIKROW
TAHT GNIHTEMOS SI
EFIL RUO SEKAM
REISAE

Does it not really help us when all the letters are systematically written from left to right? In order to read, we can fall back on a sort of automatism. The sequence does not have to be reconstructed for each word. On a simpler level you can also imagine this for a systematic left–right organization of the work. The young person with autism can fall back on an automatism in the recognition of duration and organization: there is less that has to be 'deduced', the intention is directly observable.

Figure 10. The kitchen scenario in pictorial form.

When all the symbols of the work schedule have disappeared, the work is finished. At every turn the underlying principles are the same. A person with autism has difficulty understanding or retaining abstractions in his memory (duration, time, the length represented by numbers) and so we change these 'concepts' into perception equivalents (they now 'see' the length, the duration). The weak side (abstract temporal information) is replaced by the strong side (visuospatial information). What they learn in the classroom will later be very important in the workshop. The adult will see the duration (from pictures, colours, numbers) and carry on working independently instead of being dependent on verbal instructions from the work supervisor, which are difficult for him to memorize.

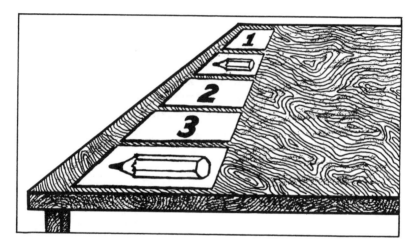

Figure 11. A work scenario

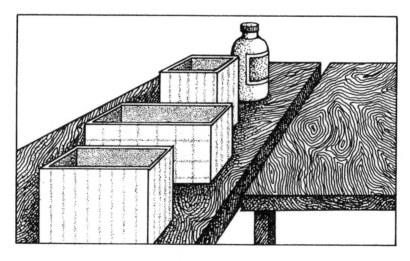

Figure 12. A work schedule on an object level.

Communication

In the preceding chapter, mention was made that communication for people with autism need not necessarily be in the form of words. The form of communication must be individualized, i.e. adapted to the individual level of abstraction. This can not only be through the medium of spoken words but also with objects, by body language, gestures, pictures, photos, or written or printed words. When selecting the appropriate form of communication, the first consideration should not be, 'let us try a form of communication which is most similar to our own' (as abstract as possible), but rather, 'let us start with the form of communication which he can handle best, as independently as possible'.

This chapter does not offer the scope to address each form of communication separately. Accordingly, preference is given to dealing with one aspect which raises the largest number of questions within the patient care system and which also links up with the central theme of the power of abstraction. This is the need for augmentative communication (communication with visual support) for verbal people with autism. Anyone who understands echolalia in autism also has a good understanding of the need for visual support.

You could say that communication is:

1. Something between two persons (communication is 'social').
2. An exchange of symbols which are universally recognizable (usually in the form of 'words'). This exchange has the intention of causing an interesting effect (one receives attention and information is exchanged).

About half of all people with autism do not speak, or they do have words but do not really understand the meaning of them, so they can be supported with forms of communication which are more concrete, more visuospatial.

People with autism, for instance, are frequently not sufficiently aware that there are means by which the environment can be influenced. The intention to achieve communication is inadequately developed. They do not understand the purpose of communication. Words are just words, pictures just pictures and objects just objects. The purpose that these symbols have in communication must be learned separately.

In order to exchange symbols with other people, you must of course also be able to understand people — as will be mentioned briefly later in this book: the social world is sometimes incomprehensible for people with autism. Some of them do not even understand the meaning of objects and in such cases this skill must be learned first. The intermediate steps which this entails are beyond the scope of this introduction. Nevertheless, the information about the visualization of time (in the preceding chapter) contributes to this. Compare it with the development of language: everyone knows that children first understand words before they actually start to speak them.

Before people with autism use pictures or objects to communicate, they must also first learn the meaning of these pictures and objects. In autism classes or communities, they learn that pictures/objects precede certain events, that pictures/objects therefore 'mean' something. Offering them the experience of a predictable environment and predictable time and events means that you are creating a good basis from which communication can start to grow.

In the preceding chapter we drew attention to the potential difficulties of people with autism in dealing with very abstract transient information. Teachers therefore try to use forms of communication which appeal to their strong visuospatial skills. In that way they can learn to communicate by making use of three-dimensional objects, two-dimensional illustrations (pictures or photos), and written or printed words.

The additional use of body language and iconic gestures (where there is a visible similarity between the symbol and the meaning) is also encouraged. Systematized sign language, such as that used by people with impaired hearing, can offer an alternative only in exceptional cases since this language is also very abstract, usually too abstract (just as words) for someone with autism. It is logical that you help someone with a literal mind-set less than you hope if you replace verbal abstractions with visual ones.

All people with autism should be able to communicate in one way or another. The 50% who are unable to speak can learn to use a less abstract form of communication. However, the 50% who are able to speak can also often be helped. With good results, through the medium of visual support. This is addressed in more detail elsewhere in this book (Peeters, 1991).

Self-help and domestic skills

Self-help and domestic skills are of course important in an educational process. The greater the ability of someone with autism to help himself, the less dependent he is on others and the more chances he has of being placed in the type of facility that offers him the best opportunities. It is a very wide-ranging area of education, in which the patient is taught hygiene, how to dress and undress himself, to eat, do the shopping, how to get from one place to another, how to deal with objects, maintenance of the garden, clothing, the home, etc.

Before we teach these skills we make analyses, we want to know what intermediate steps they entail. In an examination we determine which steps an individual with autism has already mastered and where we can help him with visual support. Take for instance 'making coffee'. We try to visualize a concept like 'making coffee'. After all, for a person with autism, 'knowing' is often equivalent to 'seeing'. This visual support is therefore a sort of scenario that we devise in order to compensate for the deficit of internal scenarios.

The abstractness of this scenario will depend on the individual. For a skill such as 'cleaning the floor', a written scenario, a picture scenario or an object scenario can be made (see Figures 13, 14 and 15).

Figure 13. 'I take my brush, I sweep the dirt into a heap'.

Examples of dressing scenarios are given in Figures 16 and 17.

Visual aids are not usually permanent. Once a person with autism can perform the necessary operations, words or pictures or objects can gradually be eliminated. Nevertheless, when visual support is taken away one should proceed with caution. After a while this knowledge may fade, now that the steps can no longer be 'seen' so that some independence is lost and the person with autism once again becomes more dependent on verbal or physical help. After all, one would not be quick to take a hearing-aid away from a person with impaired hearing and expect the user to try harder to do better. Taking away visual aids too quickly verges on (perhaps unintentional) intolerance. We must learn to accept people with autism for what they really are, instead of for what we want from them to be (more like us).

Work skills and work behaviour

The time is past when people thought that someone with autism was happy if he could play with a piece of string all day, or was left to his own devices in his own little world. People with autism are happiest when they have suitably adapted work to do. It gives everyone a good feeling to feel competent. No one likes to feel that he has nothing to do.

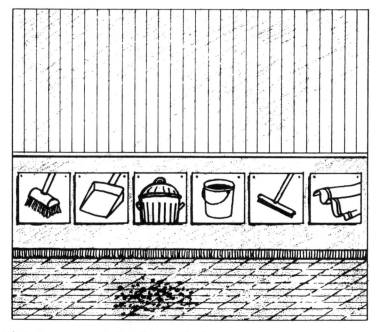

Figure 14. A picture scenario for cleaning the floor.

Figure 15. An object scenario for cleaning the floor.

Figure 16. A picture scenario for dressing.

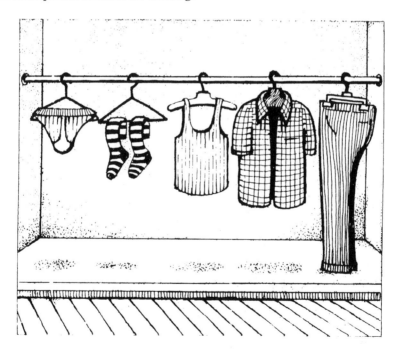

Figure 17. An object scenario for dressing.

For someone with autism, competence and success are unthinkable without clarity and transparency. These are offered by means of predictable space and time. The duration of work periods and activities can be visualized. Frequently, the content of each separate job also has to be made 'transparent', in order to compensate for difficulties in understanding. In other words, most people understand the finality of a job, what the end product will be, and through which intermediate steps can be done, but someone with autism is helped if he has immediately recognizable information. He has uncommon difficulty with work involving 'open-ended' tasks (what you are doing has to be analysed); the constituent parts of the work must speak for themselves, be self-evident. (Again, consider in this respect task analyses: we visualize a concept, so that the information processing, which normally calls on primarily left hemisphere strategies, now calls in part on the action of the right hemisphere — concept analysis versus observation synthesis). Information must be self-evident: on the written word level, on the picture level, on the object level, or through a combination of these levels.

In the teaching of work skills we start with the simplest tasks — tasks that are self-evident and well-visualized — which are chosen so that people with autism can experience a feeling of success and independence in the shortest time possible, a command of 'things' (people are so much more difficult). These include sorting tasks, assembly tasks, packing tasks and desk tasks. The visualized jobs must of course be adapted to the level of development. Younger people must be 'ripe' for them. A six-months-old normal child is not 'motivated' to do a jigsaw puzzle, his brain is not yet ready for it. By the same token, people with autism are likewise not 'motivated' to do certain tasks which call on 'thought strategies' for which their brain is not yet ready.

Some self-evident tasks for different levels of development are shown in Figure 18.

It is often claimed that people with autism are potentially the best workers. Once they have mastered a job, they are sticklers for perfection. They often enjoy repeating the same work that they do well, they have the lowest absenteeism rate and often like to carry on working, even during breaks, weekends and holidays. Sometimes, however, they risk losing their job because they display such maladjusted work behaviour. Frequently, they are not well prepared to develop good work behaviour which comprises, among other things, respecting time, asking for help if necessary, working neatly and not being too readily distracted, being amenable to change and keeping oneself occupied during breaks. Problems with 'work behaviour' which are related to lack of clarity and which can be treated in the educational domain, include the following.

1. Protests and refusals can often be avoided if the autistic worker has a daily schedule which shows what he has to do and what follows immediately after the work.
2. Problems with loss of concentration can be avoided if the work area is adequately demarcated.

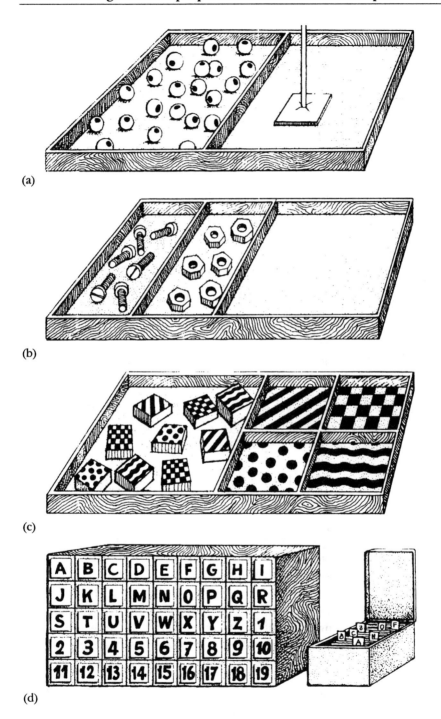

(a)

(b)

(c)

(d)

Figure 18. Tasks for different levels of development. (a) Threading beads on to a stick. (b) Screwing a nut on to a bolt and placing it on the right. (c) Sorting four different objects. (d) Sorting word pictures by their first letter.

3. Problems with lack of motivation can be kept within bounds or avoided if he is given sufficient predictability by means of a work schedule: how many tasks should he do?

Good organization of the work also plays a major role in avoiding behavioural problems. A visually supportive work organization gives a concrete answer to the very abstract question 'how?'. How does the person with autism organize his work? Offering a good work organization neatly illustrates how the 'happiness' of someone with autism depends to a considerable extent on the way in which we adjust ourselves to his handicap. For example, a person with autism has to pack biscuits and provide the bag with a label and eyelet for sealing the bag (see Figure 19).

Figure 19. Biscuit-packing task without numerical organization.

Although the intermediate steps cannot be seen, we can deduce them because we know the purpose of the activity. A person with autism needs a more direct form of information. However, visual support in itself is not enough. It must be sufficiently individualized.

The visualization in Figure 20 is certainly not clear enough for me. My brain is not ripe for it. The visual support is insufficiently individualized.

To return to the task of packing biscuits, Figure 21 shows the same boxes as Figure 20, with numbers, not in the correct sequence. This is a step in the right direction: the sequence is specified by numbers. But is it of any help to someone who doesn't know that 3 follows 2 and 2 follows 1? This is still not right.

Figure 22 provides tremendous visual support. On the table there are now areas with the numbers 1 to 5. Each time the sequence of steps to be carried out as part of a task is important, we have provided the various small boxes in the large work box with the same numbers. In that way the person with autism does not have to understand the meaning of the

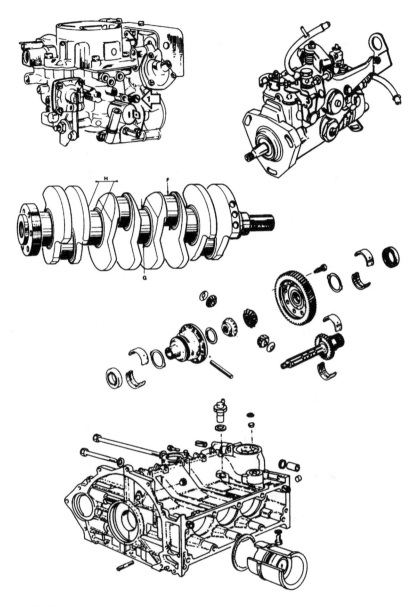

Figure 20. Visual support may not be suitable for the individual.

numbers, he only has to see them clearly. If he now places 1 on 1, 2 on 2, 3 on 3, etc. then everything will automatically be in the correct sequence and he can start work.

Variations on this theme are possible, such as a grid with various colours or motifs on the workbench (see Figure 23). The work boxes then have the same code. Colour by colour, or motif by motif the work is organized of its own accord in the correct sequence.

Figure 21. Biscuit-packing task with numerical organization, not in sequence.

Figure 22. Biscuit-packing task, organized according to numerical correspondence.

Organizing work with numbers and colours is two-dimensional, but for a number of people with autism work organization will have to be offered in three dimensions, i.e. on an object level.

In the case of the task organization in Figures 24 and 25 the worker with autism does not even need to do the 'unpacking' himself. He has a 'one-box job'. He simply takes the work box and everything is already

Figure 23. Biscuit-packing task, organized according to motifs.

organized for him. This helps to avoid failure and boost his sense of self-esteem. Naturally, he did learn beforehand to work from left to right.

The great advantage of such a fixed work organization is that very many tasks can be organized in the same way. Thus a person with autism can always fall back on a familiar routine, and he doesn't have to learn a new organization for each new task.

In this way quite a few potential behavioural problems can be 'treated' educationally, or avoided at work. However, it does call for considerable imagination and work on the part of the teacher to put himself in the position, or rather the concrete world, of a person with autism and devise adaptations to make life happier.

Everybody wants to be appreciated for what he does. Why do we work? In reality, we do almost nothing for nothing. We work for reasons of idealism, for social status, for the money. It is important to realize that most of these 'rewards' are fairly abstract and not very motivating for most people with autism. If we do not want them to gain the impression that they are having to do everything 'for nothing', then we shall have to figure out rewards which are valuable to them. That means we need to find some form of concrete reward which is relevant to the person with autism. If lemonade is all they find rewarding, then lemonade will be the reward. Examples of concrete and abstract rewards are given in Figures 26 and 27.

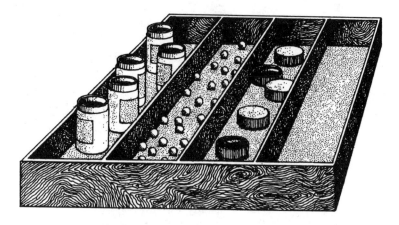

Figure 24. One-box task in several steps. Filling and closing a jar.

Figure 25. One-box task in several steps. Filling envelopes, affixing and postmarking a stamp.

Normal people and mentally retarded people without autism have many reasons for 'learning to work': they want to please mum and dad, they want their smile, they want to be like them. But this 'internal motivation' is at a fairly abstract social level, aiming too high for most people with autism. It may be necessary to start with an 'external motivation', a concrete motivator. One should move from concrete to abstract, because the other direction simply does not work.

Leisure skills

It seems somewhat contradictory that you have to teach someone skills for his 'free' time; surely you then do as you please? However, for people with autism the skills needed to spend free time (breaks, weekend, holidays) do not come spontaneously.

Figure 26. An example of a reward in concrete form.

Figure 27. An example of a reward in abstract form.

I once asked the father of a child with autism, 'What does it really mean for you, having an autistic child at home?' He said, 'My child arrives home from school at about five o'clock. If we are lucky, he is in bed by 11. Each day I ask myself, "How can I survive between five and 11?"'. There are problems with 'free time'.

Once again time must be visualized. Activities must have a visible beginning, duration and end; normal leisure activities are too 'open-ended'. To be able to choose freely, the options must be known. The options must first be visualized on object or picture or written language level. Frequently, someone with autism must literally 'learn' to choose. And he must also learn not always to choose the same. Working is often much more relaxing. Do you remember the difficulties Herman had with his free time? For a person with autism, the distinction between work time and free time is artificial. I once prepared a leisure activity for someone with autism which I had announced with a 'leisure card' on his daily schedule. However, because he had not mastered the activity he protested that this was 'work' and I ought to have made the announcement with a 'work card'. The problems involved may be so overwhelming that parents and teachers take steps to organize free time, not for every minute of the day, naturally, but in the distribution of organized and non-organized free time you often see a clear developmental trend.

Initially the life of a person with autism is so chaotic that you devote all your energy to making just a few moments or minutes transparent and predictable. These are the first 'work sessions' in which the first forms of work skills and work behaviour are taught. Those few minutes of attention demand so much concentration and effort that you can hardly ask for more. Much of the remaining time is 'free', but chaotic. This cannot be helped. (You could also formulate it like this: the many stereotyped behaviours which they have in the non-organized time are frequently a question of reflex-like behaviours under the control of the lower brain structures. As they learn to work independently and concentrate on essential matters, the activities come under the control of higher brain structures and you see the stereotyped behaviours diminish or disappear altogether. But those intellectual efforts must be in measured doses; you cannot ask too much, you must take a person with autism as and where he is. The rest of the time he 'relapses' again into stereotyped behaviour.) However, the longer a person with autism works independently, at a given moment you see that he really begins to ask, through difficult behaviours, for more organized free time. Too long periods spent in non-organized sessions land them in difficulties. Their difficult behaviour communicates that. Then it is time to start to make a clear distinction between work time and organized and non-organized free time.

The mother of an autistic child, Bart, actually times how long Bart can keep himself occupied on his own without difficulties. This is about 20 minutes, then he has a behavioural crisis and it takes several minutes for him to calm down again. His mother is tired of constantly having her life, and that of her family, ruled by these crises and wishes to put more effort into prevention. Having thought about the problem she sets the kitchen timer at 18 minutes, i.e. to ring just before the start of the difficult period. She plays a game with Bart and then he is ready for the next 20 minutes. Again she sets the kitchen timer at 18 minutes, and so on. Naturally, it demands organization, but it is worth the effort. The end result is that life is now much more enjoyable both for her and the rest of the family, and for Bart. The combination of work time, organized and non-organized free time can be represented approximately as shown in Figure 28.

Leisure skills are truly functional skills. Later, in an institution or a hostel or at work, there will always be moments and periods of non-organized free time when no activities are arranged and the person with autism will have to keep himself occupied without assistance.

During organized free time, people with autism are offered activities or work in approximately the same way as during work sessions. A special area is provided, just as previously for work, so that the sort of activity and the expected behaviour have a more predictable character. Pupils with

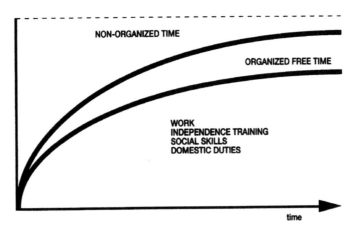

NON-ORGANIZED TIME

ORGANIZED FREE TIME

WORK
INDEPENDENCE TRAINING
SOCIAL SKILLS
DOMESTIC DUTIES

time

Figure 28. The combination of work time and organized and non-organized free time.

autism also use visual support during these free-time sessions, which gives an answer to questions such as, 'When?', 'How long?' and 'How?'. In addition, of course, they continue to have non-organized time, but in carefully measured doses, each according to his need. Figures 29 and 30 show some activities which are organized in approximately the same way as work tasks, only the materials are associated by us with free time. Whereas most leisure activities for normal children are fairly open-ended, these tasks speak for themselves.

Visual support can also have its practical uses in all sorts of motor activities. People with autism are often unable to take part in PE exercises ('they cannot imitate you, they don't stand where they're supposed to, they don't understand what is expected of them, they follow me around all the time, etc.'). Nevertheless, clarification about the start, duration and end of activities can boost motivation considerably.

Figure 29. You immediately see how the pieces fit together; the perception speaks for itself.

Figure 30. What do you do with toy cars? The intention has to be deduced.

Take, for instance, the PE exercise in Figure 31. Your first thought may be 'I can never motivate my pupil to do that'. But just think for a moment: the exercise as we are doing it — arms behind the head and then bending forwards — seems so vague, so aimless, you don't see the point, the object. But supposing you place a number of sticks behind the person doing the exercise. Each time he bends backwards he takes a stick and places it in the box in front of him. That is a lot more concrete and one can see what the exercise is about.

Figure 31. An example of a PE exercise depicted pictorially.

Or take a running exercise, 'Run', you say. Yes, but where should he start, how long should he run for, and where to? Figure 32 shows how you can start at the flag, take a ball, run one lap and place the ball in the box. Then you take the next ball, you do the next lap, and when all the balls are gone, the exercise is finished.

Now try to visualize an exercise on a vertical ladder — climb up and down 10 times. Without visualization this seems vague and pointless. But if you have to carry objects up the ladder one at a time until they are all at the top, then the motivation (start, duration, finish are clear) is obvious (see Figure 33).We want to know why we are letting ourselves in for, and so does a person with autism.

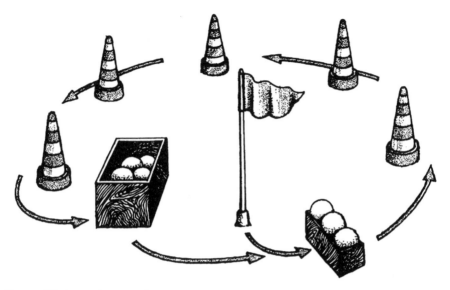

Figure 32. A running exercise.

Figure 33. An exercise to climb the ladder.

If you combine these different exercises with 'transition cards' all visualized on a level that the person with autism can understand, then you can develop a motor circuit which he can work out independently with absolutely no help from others, and with much pleasure.

Social skills

If you perform a leisure activity with two (or more) people, that constitutes a social activity. And people with autism have the greatest problems of all with social cognition. Social free time therefore creates special problems, most certainly if we improvise too much in the offering of activities. Remember that people with autism have particular difficulty with communication. Communication is something we primarily associate with speaking. But we know that people with autism often receive better help from forms of communication that require a lower abstract level: written words, photos, drawings, objects. Some people with autism remain on a so-called precommunicative level: they want to impart something, but they have not yet learned real communication and so they simply develop outbursts of anger: they want to communicate something, but no one understands them straightaway. Let us not forget that presocial levels also exist. Social interaction is something that we immediately associate (just like communication) with the highest level: reciprocity, mutual interactions. But people with autism are socially blind: comprehension of the feelings, ideas and the intentions of others demands too much analysis of meaning, it is not (sufficiently) directly perceptible. Playing, or spending free time together, is therefore often better on less abstract levels. In football, handball, etc. there are too many rules which are not directly observable. Certain forms of combined play go much more smoothly if the rules are simplified and clarified. In a game like dominoes (or cards or doing a jigsaw puzzle) the person whose turn it is can be visualized by objects or pictures. Sometimes, parallel play is the highest form of social interaction that people with autism are able to manage. And some of them have such difficulty in accepting the nearness of other people that they stay on a presocial level. An example of parallel play is given in Figure 34, and an example of turn-taking play in Figure 35.

Figure 34. Parallel play.

Figure 35. Turn-taking play. An object (the box) is pushed to and fro to indicate whose turn it is.

A number of social skills are of a practical nature and revolve round the border area between self-help and social skills: they might be called social self-help (eating properly, greeting people, making use of public transport, etc.). The problem is, however, that 'self-help aspects' cannot be completely isolated from mutual social aspects, they melt into one another, without clear boundary lines. When you meet someone you should immediately be able to 'read' his status, his plans; you must be able to empathize with his perspective and take this into account. People are so unpredictable and so difficult to a person with autism. The psychologist Jerome Bruner called social behaviour 'abstract symbols in perpetual motion' (Bruner, 1973).

Social cognition, knowing and understanding mutual social behaviour, is the most difficult of all. People with autism sometimes feel like 'an alien without a reference map'. Or, in the words of Temple Grandin, 'like an anthropologist on the planet Mars'.

We can visualize quite a lot of social situations by making a sort of job analysis of social behaviour in its various guises (by means of written words, drawings, photos, video cassettes), but there are always some aspects which are too subtle or changeable and depend upon the context. One of the new ways to try to teach social behaviour consists of offering certain social scenarios. As before, there is insufficient 'inner language ' — an inner scenario — so attempts are made through visual support to design external scenarios by way of compensation).

In social scenarios, parents and professionals give answers to the questions 'Who?', 'Where?', 'When?', and 'Why?' (Gray, 1993), and this gives people with autism a better chance of 'reading' social situations.

The scenarios may be descriptive, such as:

The bell sounds when playtime is over.
The children stand in line in front of the door.
They wait until the teacher comes.

The scenarios may also indicate the expected behaviour:

I can hear the bell.
I stop what I am doing.
I go and stand in line.
I shall wait for the teacher.

Or the scenarios may be a combination of both:

The bell sounds when playtime is over.
I can hear the bell.
I stop what I am doing.
The children stand in line in front of the door.
I go and stand in line.
They are waiting until the teacher comes.
I shall wait for the teacher.

Social scenarios are also used to prepare people with autism for a future change, or to tell them most emphatically what sort of behaviour is expected from them in that situation.

When I drive home with mummy, I shall put the seat belt on.
I will not scream if the car stops at a red traffic light.
I shall rest my hands quietly on my knees.

For a person with autism, it is then much easier to behave 'politely', 'properly', because often when he is troublesome he does not really intend to be negative. (The term 'negativism' should be reserved for deliberate refusals to carry out instructions which are known to have been understood.) He often does not 'understand' the expected behaviour because, after all, he has not 'seen' it.

Conclusions

Words such as 'training' and 'education' are part of the technical jargon and sometimes come over as somewhat cool, neutral and detached.

Nevertheless, the aim is to improve quality of life. We frequently ask parents how we should help their children to be as happy as possible when they are older. The answers given correspond exactly to the aims of the educational programme and training package.

As visual support plays such an important role, we can call training and education specialized in autism 'augmentative' (giving support). This is analogous to 'augmentative communication', the development of supportive communication for those who are unable to express themselves verbally, or only with difficulty. Augmentative or supportive training and education, therefore, is the most important *modus operandi* for the prevention of behavioural problems.

Unfortunately, one of the many associated problems of people with autism is that quite a few have defective vision, and some are blind. For them, a tactile approach should as far as possible replace the visual approach. And people with autism who are not (yet) able to make use of the lowest abstraction level, namely object scenarios, have to rely totally on physical help.

It is regrettable to have to conclude that the people with autism who are most in need of help are the most difficult ones to help (their low mental age prevents them from understanding information on a picture level). Even 'demonstrating' may not be helpful because they may have acquired too few imitation skills to mimic our model. Frequently, the only possible learning strategy still open is continuing physical guidance. Alternatively, many can also learn through individual coaching sessions to understand the relationship between an object and a picture. There is nearly always something that they can learn. On the other hand, people with autism with greater intellectual capabilities will often become progressively less dependent on visual support.

Epilogue

Autism is recognized as a 'pervasive developmental disorder' by the whole of the scientific community. Asperger syndrome and some of the other autistic-like conditions do not necessarily infer 'pervasive' problems. Nevertheless, everyone agrees about the profundity, the seriousness of the impairments: someone with a restricted ability to understand communication and social behaviour, and who himself has such problems with the development of imagination that he can add little meaning to observation, is indeed profoundly affected. But are people with autism also being 'pervasively helped'?

For very many, the answer is still 'no'. Nevertheless, the quality of life of people with autism depends to a large extent on the way in which teachers, carers and others understand their handicap and are able to adapt the environment, and their style of communication, to them. The overriding condition for that is the training and education of everybody involved in the helping and teaching of people with autism.

He finds it difficult to 'read' our eyes, gestures, postures. He finds it difficult to understand what we think, what we feel and what our intentions are. He is too much of a 'behaviourist', he finds it difficult to transcend the literal, to see the meaning behind behaviours. From the social point of view, he seems to be blind.

This is all quite normal for someone with autism. However, for a teacher who does not understand autism, such behaviours are not normal: just like parents, he feels rejected, not understood, unrewarded, and he may think, 'What an egoist, what a horrible little monster; well now, I'll soon put an end to that, you see if I don't'. Thus someone is punished because he is handicapped — and as we know: usually without any favourable result for, as we also know, reward and punishment are experienced by a person with autism in a very individual way.

Parents often observe that professionals who are working with their children do not think of training until a crisis situation is reached, when the behaviour really becomes too difficult. In this way, training is a sort of post-training, an 'emergency breakdown system'. Everywhere in Europe there is still a very long way to go in the establishment of a full-scale 'pre-training' curriculum.

The problems of autism can be regarded as a threefold problem of imagination:

1. For the person with autism: the handicap is essentially a problem of imagination, i.e., of the ability to transcend the literal.
2. For carers and parents: autism is a problem of imagination, because it is so difficult to enter into that other, more concrete world, a world of a lower symbolic level.
3. For the policy makers: autism is a problem of imagination, because 'they haven't experienced it themselves'. When they listen to the desiderata of parents and carers in connection with the resources that are needed to improve the quality of life of autistic fellow-citizens, they often think that they are exaggerating.

Since policy makers know the theoretical definition of autism, but not the practical consequences in everyday life, they do not have sufficient understanding (translated into resources) of the perplexity and exhaustion of parents and carers who are receiving insufficient help.

Professional training and education specialized in autism call for appropriate resources. These should be allocated by the political establishment. In this respect, autism is not only an educational problem, but above all, a political one.

References

Akerley M (1988) What's in a Name? In Schopler E, Mesibov G (Eds) Diagnosis and assessment in autism. New York: Plenum Press.

American Psychiatric Association (1994) Diagnostic and Statistical Manual of Mental Disorders. Fourth edition. Washington, DC: APA.

Asperger H (1944) Die autistischen Psychopathen im Kindesalter. Archiv für Psychiatrie und Nervenkrankheiten. 117:76–136.

Baron-Cohen S (1995) Mindblindness. Massachusetts, MA: MIT Press.

Bettelheim B (1967) The Empty Fortress: Infantile autism and the birth of self. London: Collier-Macmillan.

Bleuler E (1911) Dementia Praecox or the Group of Schizophrenias. Wenen. Translated by J. Zinkin. New York: International University Press.

Bruner J (1973) Beyond the Information Given. London: Allen & Unwin.

Crawford J (1992) A Handbook of Neuropsychological Assessment. Hove: Lawrence Erlbaum Associates.

Dewey M (1983) Parental Perspective of Needs. In Schopler E, Mesibov G (Eds) Autism in Adolescents and Adults. New York: Plenum Press.

Fay W, Schuler A (1980) Emerging language in Autistic Children. Baltimore: University Park Press.

Fredericks B *et al.* (1983) The Education needs of the autistic adolescent. In Schopler E, Mesibov G (Eds) Autism in Adolescents and Adults. New York: Plenum Press.

Frith U (1989) Autism. Explaining the Enigma. Oxford: Basil Blackwell.

Frith U (Ed) (1991) Autism and Asperger Syndrome. Cambridge: Cambridge University Press.

Gazzaniga MS (1970) The Bisected Brain. New York: Appleton.

Gillberg C (1983) Perceptual, motor and attentional deficits in Swedish primary school children. Some child psychiatric aspects. Journal of Child Psychology and Psychiatry. 24: 377–403.

Gillberg C (1985), Asperger's syndrome and recurrent psychosis case study. Journal of Autism and Developmental Disorders. 15: 389–397.

Gillberg C (1989) Asperger syndrome in 23 Swedish children. Developmental Medicine and Child Neurology. 31: 520–531.

Gillberg C (1991) Clinical and neurobiological aspects of Asperger syndrome in six family studies. In Frith U (Ed) Autism and Asperger Syndrome. Cambridge: Cambridge University Press.

Gillberg C, Coleman M (1992) The Biology of the Autistic Syndromes. Clinics in Developmental Medicine No 126. 2nd edition. London, New York: Mac Keith Press.

Gillberg C, Persson E, Grufman M, Themnér U (1986) Psychiatric disorders in mildly and severely mentally retarded urban children and adolescents: epidemiological aspects. British Journal of Psychiatry. 149: 68–74.

Gillberg I C, Gillberg C (1989) Asperger syndrome — some epidemiological considerations: a research note. Journal of Child Psychology and Psychiatry. 30: 631–638.

Grandin T (1992) An inside view of autism. In Schopler E, Mesibov G. (Eds) High Functioning Individuals with Autism. New York: Plenum Press.

Grandin T, Scariano M (1986) Emergence Labelled Autistic. Novato: Arena Press.

Gray C (1993) The Social Story Book. Jeuson MI: Jenison Public Schools.

Halliday M (1973) Explorations in the Functions of Language. London: Edward Arnold.

Happé F (1994) Autism. An Introduction to Psychological Theory. London: UCL Press.

Haracopos D, Kelstrup A (1975) Psychotic behaviour in children under the institutions for the mentally retarded in Denmark. Journal of Autism and Childhood Schizophrenia. 8: 1–12.

Hermelin B (1976) Coding and the sense modalities. In Wing L (Ed) Early Childhood Autism. Oxford: Pergamon Press.

Joliffe T, Lansdown R, Robinson C (1992) Autism: A Personal Account. Communication. 26: 3.

Kanner L (1943) Autistic disturbances of affective contact. Nervous Child. 2: 217–250.

Leslie A M (1987) Pretense and representations: the origins of 'theory of mind'. Psychological Review. 94: 412.

McHale S, Gamble W (1986) Mainstreaming handicapped children in public school settings: challenges and limitations. In Schopler E, Mesibov G (Eds) Social Behavior in Autism. New York: Plenum Press.

Mesibov G (1988) Diagnosis and assessment of autistic adolescents and adults. In Schopler E, Mesibov G (Eds) Diagnosis and Assessment in Autism. New York: Plenum Press.

Mesibov G, Troxler M, Boswell S (1988) Assessment in the classroom. In Schopler E, Mesibov G (Eds) Diagnosis and Assessment in Autism. New York: Plenum Press.

Peeters T (1987) Autisme Vanaf de Adolescentie. Nijmegen: Dekker en van de Vegt.

Peeters T (1991) Autisme en visualisering. In Ondersteunde communicatie: een neurolinguistische benadering. Symposium Belgische Beroepsvereniging van Neurolinguisten en ISAAC. Antwerpen: VIA.

Peeters T (1992) The training of professionals in autism. Proceedings of the 4th congress Autism-Europe, Den Haag.

Peeters T (1984) Uit zichzelf gekeerd. Nijmegen: Dekker en van de Vegt.

Peeters T (1994) Autisme. Van begrijpen tot begeleiden. Antwerpen: Hadewych.

Peeters T (1997) Autism. From theoretical understanding to educational intervention. London: Whurr.

Prizant B (1984) Language acquisition and communicative behavior in autism. In Prizant B (Ed) Seminars in Speech and Language 4: 63.

Prizant B, Schuler A (1987) Facilitating Communication: Language approaches. In Cohen D, Donnellan A (Eds) Handbook of Autism and Pervasive Developmental Disorders. New York: Wiley.

Rourke et al. (1983) Child Neuropsychology. New York: The Gilford Press.

Rutter M, Schopler E (1987) Autism and pervasive developmental disorders. Concepts and diagnostic issues. Journal of Autism and Developmental Disorders. 17: 159.

Schopler, Reichler and Lansing (1981) Teaching Strategies for Parents and Professionals. Baltimore MD: University Park Press.

Schopler E, Mesibov G (1988) Introduction to diagnosis and assessment in autism. In Schopler E, Mesibov G (Eds) Diagnosis and Assessment in Autism. New York: Plenum Press.

Schopler E, Reichler R (1979) Psychoeducational Profile. Baltimore: University Park Press.

Steffenburg S (1990) Neurobiological Correlates of Autism: University of Göteborg.

Steffenburg S, Gillberg C (1986) Autism and autistic-like conditions in Swedish rural and urban areas: a population study. British Journal of Psychiatry. 149: 81–87.

Tantam D (1988) Asperger's syndrome. Journal of Child Psychology and Psychiatry. 29: 245–255.

Volkmar F (1986) Compliance, non-compliance and negativism. In Schopler E, Mesibov G (Eds) Social Behavior in Autism. New York: Plenum Press.

WHO (1993) International Classification of Diseases and Disorders (ICD-10). Geneva: WHO.

Wing L (1981) Asperger's syndrome: a clinical account. Psychological Medicine. 11: 115–129.

Wing L (1989) The diagnosis of autism. In Gillberg C (Ed) Diagnosis and Treatment of Autism. New York: Plenum Press.

Wing L, Gould J (1979) Severe impairments of social interaction and associated abnormalities in children: epidemiology and classification. Journal of Autism and Developmental Disorders. 9: 11–29.

Index

absence spells, 51
abstraction, level of, 64
  objects, 67–68
  pictures/drawings/photos, 66–67
  spoken word, 65
  written/printed word, 65–66
active, odd style, 18, 21–22
adaptation of environment to autism, 77–78
adolescence, 18, 21
adulthood, 18, 21–22
aggression, 29
aitalopram, 57
Akerley, M., 71–72
aloof-autistic style, 18, 21–22
alternative signification, 78
American Psychiatric Association, 27
amygdala, 45, 46
Angelman syndrome, 43
antidepressants, 57
anti-epileptic anti-convulsive drugs, 51, 57–58
aphasia, 42
Asperger, Hans, 24, 30
Asperger syndrome, 24–25
  associated factors
    epilepsy, 41
    mental retardation, 41, 50
    visual problems, 42
  brain dysfunction, 45, 46, 47
  early brain damage, 44
  heredity, 44
  incidence, 39
    gender differences, 40
  medical diagnosis, 30–34
  differential, 36
  IQ levels, 36–37
  motor clumsiness, 25, 31, 32, 54
  neuropsychological testing, 38, 39
  outcome, 26
  stereotypic behaviour, 23
assessment of autism, 77
atypical depression, 36
auditory brain stem response (ABR)
  examination, 45, 53, 54
auditory hyper- or hyposensitivity, 29
autistic continuum, 30
autistic-like conditions, 26
  associated factors
    epilepsy, 41
    mental retardation, 41
  incidence, 39, 40
  IQ levels, 37
  medical diagnosis, 34
autism spectrum disorders, 30
autistic traits
  incidence, 39
  medical diagnosis, 35
avoidant gaze
  fragile X syndrome, 55
  preschool years, 20
awareness training, 79–80
AZART, 6–7

babbling, 15
back problems, 53
Baron-Cohen, S., 71
Bart, 106
behavioural impairment, 22
  Asperger syndrome, 25, 33

medical diagnosis
    of Asperger syndrome, 33
    of autism, 27, 28, 29
overall restriction of behavioural
    repertoire, 24
stereotypies and stereotypic behav-
    iour, 22–24
benzodiazepine, 50, 58
Bettelheim, B., 9
biochemical signs of brain dysfunction,
    44–45
biological basis of autism, 41, 45–46,
    47
    associated syndromes, 41–42
    morphological and biochemical
    signs of brain dysfunction, 44–45
    possible causal factors, 43–44
    provisional synthesis, 46–47
Bleuler, Eugen, viii
blindness, 42, 52
Block Design test, 38
blood tests, 47
body contact, 20
body language, 94
body rocking, 22
bonding, 20
bone problems, 53
boys, 40
brain
    early damage, 44
    frontal lobes, 43, 45, 46
    left vs. right sides, 2–3
        echolalia, 4, 5
    morphological and chemical signs of
    dysfunction, 44–46
    temporal lobes
        dysfunction, 43, 44, 45, 46, 53
        epilepsy, 41
brain stem dysfunction, 45, 46, 53–54
Bruner, Jerome, 78, 111

carbamazepine, 58–59
carer profile, 82–84.
CAT scans, 44
causal factors, possible
    early brain damage, 44
    heredity, 43–44
    medical disorders, 43
Center for Training on Autism, 80
central coherence, 46

neuropsychological testing, 37, 38
central stimulants, 58
cerebellar dysfunction, 44, 45, 46, 54
cerebrospinal fluid, 45
chaos, 49
childhood disintegrative disorder, 28
    medical diagnosis, 34
        differential, 36
clapping, 22
clonazepam, 58
clozapine, 57
clumsiness, 54
    Asperger syndrome, 25, 31, 32
collecting, 23
communication impairment, 10–11, 15
    adulthood, 18
    Asperger syndrome, 25, 30, 31, 32
    education and guidance, 93–94
    first year, 15–16
    medical diagnosis
        of Asperger syndrome, 30, 31, 32
        of autism, 27, 28, 29
    pre-adolescence and adolescence,
    18
    preschool years, 16–17
    school years, 17
    social skills, 110
    training professionals and parents,
    73
complex-partial seizure epilepsy, 41
Comprehension test, 38
computed axial tomography (CAT)
    scans, 44
concentration, 98

daily schedules, 87–88, 89
DAMP, 35
deafness, 42
decoupling, 7, 67
deficits in attention, motor control and
    perception (DAMP), 35
delayed echolalia, 3, 4, 68
depression, 35, 36
deprivation, 35
developmental disorder, autism as,
    14–15
    Asperger syndrome, 24–25
    behaviour and imagination impair-
    ment, 22–24
    communication impairment, 15–18

outcome, 26
significant developmental scales,
    9–14
social impairments, 18–22
Dewey, M., 84
diagnosis, *see* differential diagnosis;
    medical diagnosis
Diagnostic and Statistical Manual
    (DSM), 27
    see also DSM-IV
diazepam, 58
differential diagnosis
    deprivation and depression, 35
    mental retardation, 35
    schizophrenia, 35–36
    specific problems
        Asperger syndrome, 36
        childhood disintegrative
        disorder, 36
disintegrative psychosis, *see* childhood
    disintegrative disorder
disturbed time concept, 49
DNA tests, 47
domestic skills, 94–95, 96
dopamine-breakdown products, 45, 46
Downís syndrome, 39
drawings, 66–67
Droste, 6
DSM-IV
    Asperger syndrome, 30, 33
    autism, 27, 28
    autistic-like conditions, 34, 37
    childhood disintegrative disorder,
    34
dysphasia, 42, 52

ear problems, 42
eating habits, 29
echo-behaviour, 81
echolalia, 3–5, 81
    adolescence, 18
    delayed, 3, 4, 68
    preschool years, 16
    school years, 17
echo-play, 81
echopraxia, 81
EEGs, 45
egocentricity, 24
elbows in maximal flexion, 22
electroencephalograms, 45
empathy, 33–34, 46

neuropsychological testing, 37, 38,
    39
environment, adaptation to autism,
    77–78
environmental toxins, 43
epilepsy
    associated with autism, 41, 50–51
    incidence, 40
    medication, 57–58
    Moebius syndrome, 56
    outcome, 26
    partial tetrasomy 15 syndrome, 56
    tuberous sclerosis, 55
Ergenyl, 57
ethical code, need for, 81
examination of patients, 77
executive functions, 46
    neuropsychological testing, 37, 39
eye-contact 20
eye-poking, 23
eyes
    abnormal movements, 42, 45, 51
    impaired vision, 42, 45, 51–52
eye tests, 47

face-hitting, 23
facial expression
    Asperger syndrome, 25
    Moebius syndrome, 56
fetal damage, 43
finger-flicking, 22
finger tapping, 23
finger traction, 23
first year, 15–16, 18–19
fluoxetine, 57
fluvoxamine, 57
follow-up, 81–82
fragile X syndrome, 55
    as causal factor, 43
    eye-contact, avoidance of, 20
    joint problems, 53
    genital malformations, 53
    tests, 47
free time, 104–110
freezing of body, 22–23
frontal lobes, 43, 45, 46
functional skills, 78–79

gangliosides, 45, 46
gaze
    Asperger syndrome, 25

fragile X syndrome, 55
preschool years, 20
tuberous sclerosis, 55
gender differences
incidence of autism, 40
Rett syndrome, 56
genetic counselling, 47
genetics, 43–44
genetic stoppage, 43
genital malformations, 53
GFA proteins, 45, 46
Gillberg, C., 30, 31
Gillberg, I. C., 30, 31
girls
incidence of autism, 40
Rett syndrome, 53, 56
glasses, 51
glial fibrillary acidic (GFA) proteins, 45, 46
Grandin, Temple, 1, 2, 66, 111
grand mal seizures, 50–51

Haldol, 57
haloperidol, 57
hand-flapping, 22
hand tapping, 23
hand-twirling, 22
hand-waving, 22
head-crashing, 23
head rotating, 22
head shaking, 22
hearing-aids, 52
hearing impairment, 42, 52
hearing tests, 47
Helier dementia, see childhood disintegration disorder
Hellerís psychosis, see childhood disintegration disorder
heredity, 43–44
Herman, 59–62, 105
Hermolepsin, 57
herpes encephalitis, 43
herpes virus infection, 44
hyperactivity
diagnosis of autism, 29
first year, 16
fragile X syndrome, 55
medication, 57
tuberous sclerosis, 55
hyperrealism, 5–8
hypersensitivity

auditory, 29
to touch, 29
hypoactivity
adolescence, 21
diagnosis of autism, 29
first year, 16
hypomelanosis of Ito, 43, 52
hyposensitivity, auditory, 29
hypotonia, 54

ICD-10
Asperger syndrome, 30, 32–33
autism, 27, 29
autistic-like conditions, 34
childhood disintegrative disorder, 34
iconic gestures, 94
imagination impairment, 7–8, 13–14, 22, 116
abstraction, 68
Jan, 64
medical diagnosis of autism, 27, 28, 29
overall restriction of behavioural repertoire, 24
stereotypies and stereotypic behaviour, 22–24
training professionals and parents, 73
incidence of autism, 39–40, 79
gender differences, 40
infantile spasms, 41
infection as causal factor, 44
intelligence, see IQ levels
interest patterns, 23
internal language, 88–89, 111
International Classification of Diseases (ICD), 27
see also ICD-10
IQ levels, 33–34, 36–37
neuropsychological testing, 37–38
and outcome, 26
see also mental retardation
Itoís hypomelanosis, 43, 52

Jan, 62–63
communication, 63
imagination and play, 64
social interaction, 63–64
Johan, 5
joint problems, 53

Kanner, L., viii, 22
Kanner syndrome, viii
kyphosis, 53

lamotrigine, 58
Landau-Kleffner syndrome, 36
language impairments, 10–11, 52
    Asperger syndrome, 25
    and outcome, 26
late onset autism, 34
learning problems, 40
leisure skills, 104–110
listing, 23
lithium, 57
love, 84
lumbar puncture, 47

magnetic resonance imaging (MRI)
    scans, 44
Magritte, Renè, 66–67
make-believe play, 5–6
Maria, 68–69
marker chromosome 15 syndrome, 53,
    56
medical diagnosis
    of autism, 27–29
    differential diagnosis, 35–36
    of disorders of autism spectrum,
    30–35
    incidence of autism, 39–40
    IQ, 36–37
    neuropsychological testing, 37–39
medical disorders as causal factor, 43
medication, 56, 58
    anti-convulsive drugs, 57–58
    antidepressants, 57
    central stimulants, 58
    lithium, 57
    neuroleptics, 57
Melleril, 57
memorizing, 23
men, 18
mental retardation, 2, 9
    associated with autism, 41, 49–50
    autistic traits, 35
    differential diagnosis, 35, 36, 37
    fragile X syndrome, 55
    incidence, 40
    Moebius syndrome, 56
    neuropsychological testing, 37
    partial tetrasomy 15 syndrome, 56

Rett syndrome, 56
    tuberous sclerosis 55–56
metabolic disorders, 43
meta-reality, 5, 6, 7
mind, theory of, 37, 39
Moebius syndrome, 53, 56
mood swings, 29
morphological signs of brain dysfunc-
    tion, 44–45
motivation, 98, 100, 104
motor clumsiness, 54
    Asperger syndrome, 25, 31, 32
motor stereotypes, 22–23
MRI scans, 44
muscle relaxants, 50
music, 54
mutism
    adulthood, 18
    preschool years, 16
    reflective, 40
    school years, 17

nerve cells, 46
neurofibromatosis, 52–53
neuroleptics, 57
neurological disorders
    as causal factor, 43
    and outcome, 26
neuropsychological testing, 37–39, 47
neurotransmitters, 45
nitrazepam, 58
noise, variable reaction to, 29
noradrenalin-breakdown products, 45

Object Assembly test, 38
objects, 67–68
open-ended tasks, 98
ophthalmologists, 51
Orap, 57
Orfiril, 57

pain, reduced sensitivity to, 20, 23
    diagnosis of autism, 29
palilalia
    adolescence, 18
    preschool years, 16
    school years, 17
parallel play, 110
paranoid personality disorder, 36
parents, see training professionals and
    parents

partial tetrasomy 15 syndrome (marker
  chromosome 15 syndrome), 53, 56
passive, friendly style, 18, 21–22
pathological demand avoidance, 40
personal pronouns, reversal of, 16–17
pervasive developmental disorders
  (PDD), 30
pervasiveness of autism, 74, 76
PET studies, 45
phenobarbital, 58
phenyl ketonuria syndrome, 43
phenytoin, 58
photos, 66–67
physical exercise (PE), 107–109
Picture Arrangement test, 38
pictures, 66–67
pimozide, 57
places, 86–87
play, 5–6, 64, 110–111
pointing, 15
positron emission tomography (PET)
  studies, 45
postnatal herpes encephalitis, 43
post-training, 81–82
Prader-Willi syndrome, 53
pre-adolescence, 18, 21
predictability, 85–87
preschool years, 16–17, 19–20
pre-training, 79–80
printed word, 65–66
professionals, *see* training professionals and parents
psychomotor epilepsy, 41
psychosis, childhood, 30

reciprocity, lack of, 19–20, 21
Rett syndrome, 28, 47, 56
  back problems, 53
  differential diagnosis, 36
rewards, 103, 105
risperidone, 57
rituals, 23, 87
  Asperger syndrome, 24
Rombouts, 6
routines, 23, 85–87
  Asperger syndrome, 24
rubella infection *in utero*, 43, 44

schedules, 87–88, 89, 90–92
schizoid personality disorder, 36
schizophrenia, viii, 30

differential diagnosis, 35–36
schizotypal disorder, 36
school years, 17, 21
scoliosis, 53
selective mutism, 40
self-destructive behaviour, 23, 54–55
  adolescence, 21
  diagnosis of autism, 29
  medication, 57
  preschool years, 20
  tuberous sclerosis, 55
self-help skills, 94–95, 97
  loss of, 21
  social, 111
semantic pragmatic disorder, 25, 36
serotonin reuptake inhibitors, 57
sign language, 52, 94
single photon emission computed
  tomography (SPECT), 45
skin abnormalities, 52–53
Smarties test, 39
social impairments, 11–13, 15, 18
  adulthood, 21–22
  Asperger syndrome, 24, 31, 32, 33
  first year, 18–19
  gender differences, 40
  Jan, 63–64
  medical diagnosis
    of Asperger syndrome, 31, 32, 33
    of autism, 27, 28, 29
  pre-adolescence and adolescence,
    21
  preschool years, 19–20
  school years, 21
  training professionals and parents,
    72–73
social scenarios, 111–112
social skills, 110–112
sound, variable reaction to, 29
special educational needs, 79
specialized training programme, 80–81
SPECT, 45
spectacles, 51
spectrum disorders, 30
speech impairments, 42, 52
spinal problems, 53
spoken word, 65
squint, 42, 45
  training, 51
stereotypic behaviour, 23–24
  leisure skills, 106

training professionals and parents,
73
stereotypies, 22–23
    adolescence, 21
    Rett syndrome, 56
Steven, 1, 2, 3
stiffening of body, 22–23
structure, need for, 49
Sven, 1, 2, 5
symbols, 89
symmetrical hand-flapping, 22
Szatmari, 32

Tegretol, 57
temporal lobes
    dysfunction, 43, 44, 45, 46, 53
    epilepsy, 41
theoretical knowledge of autism, 76–77
theory of mind, 37, 39
thigh-slapping, 23
thioridazine, 57
Thomas, 69, 81
tics, 22, 23
time, 87–92
    disturbed concept of, 49
    leisure skills, 105
    management, 78, 87
tiptoe, 23
touch, hypersensitivity to, 29
toxins, 43
training professionals and parents
    carer profile, 82–84
    communication, 73
    content, 74–79
    imagination, 73
    pervasiveness of autism, 74
    social interaction, 72–73
    special nature of autism, 71–72
    types, 79–82
traits, autistic
    incidence, 39
    medical diagnosis, 35
triad symptoms, 27
tuberous sclerosis, 47, 52, 53, 55–56

as causal factor, 43
and outcome, 26
turn-taking play, 110–111

urine tests, 47

Valium 58
valproic acid, 57–58
ventricles, brain, 44
verbal stereotypies, 23
vigabatrine, 58
visual impairments
    associated with autism, 42, 45,
    51–52
    augmentative training and educa-
    tion, 113
visual support, 68–70, 86, 113
    communication, 93–94
    kitchen programme, 90, 91
    leisure skills, 107, 108–109
    schedules, 87–88, 89, 90–92
    self-help and domestic skills, 95, 96,
    97
    training professionals and parents,
    75, 79, 80
    works skills and work behaviour,
    100–103, 104
vocal stereotypies, 23
Vygotsky, 88

walking high on tiptoe, 23
Wechsler Intelligence Scale for
    Children (WISC), 37–38
Wisconsin Card Sorting Test, 38–39
women, 18
work schedules, 90–92
work sessions, 106
work skills and work behaviour,
    95–104
World Health Organization (WHO), 27
wrist-biting, 23
written word, 65–66

XXY syndrome, 53